HECTOR BERLIOZ

HECTOR BERLIOZ

By

TOM S. WOTTON

BOOKS FOR LIBRARIES PRESS

FREEPORT, NEW YORK

First Published 1935
Reprinted 1970

STANDARD BOOK NUMBER:

8369-5306-1

LIBRARY OF CONGRESS CATALOG CARD NUMBER:

70-114902

PRINTED IN THE UNITED STATES OF AMERICA

To
MY WIFE

PREFACE

THIS book is in no wise a biography of Hector Berlioz, some knowledge of the principal events of his life being presumed to be possessed by its readers. I have planned the several chapters almost as independent essays dealing with particular aspects of the French composer's genius as a musician and behaviour as a man; and in so doing I have endeavoured to present a true picture of the master, conscious that in some ways it may differ from that existent in many minds. I claim no more authority for my ideas than that which can be obtained from a close study of his works (both musical and literary) for very many years, together with a large acquaintance with the numerous books and articles relating to him.

Misconceptions have arisen around every composer, but possibly they are greater than usual with Berlioz, because on certain points some of his admirers seem to have joined hands with his detractors. Instead of insisting that this statement is devoid of proof and that based on erroneous premises, they have been inclined to acquiesce in the probable truth of both of them, and lamely to offer apologies in place of contradictions. For instance, some of his friends are disposed to take it for granted that much of the Memoirs is a tissue of lies, and that the German edition of his musical works faithfully represents his intentions. In the following pages I shall unfortunately be compelled to draw attention to the infidelities of the latter, since it is obviously absurd to judge a musician from a faulty text. As to the former, it is sufficient to insist here that their inaccuracies have been much exaggerated. Unless a writer's memory be so phenomenal as to be suspect, he must of necessity be hazy over a multitude of details.

In many ways Berlioz has not been treated fairly. He at times has been judged by standards that would not be applied to others. Accusations have been brought against him on the evidence of a single witness, whose credentials have not been scrutinized. He has been abused for doing things that are the everyday custom of his detractors. Above all, he is too often criticized in a flippant vein which can only be paralleled in some of the early notices of Wagner's works, and in any case is in dubious taste. That the French composer should not appeal to every one is understandable. His originality and his system of harmony not being derived from keyboard practice are sufficient to make him antagonistic to some. Possibly many of the other masters are not so universally admired as is supposed. We hear little, however, from the malcontents, because they have resigned themselves to the inevitable. They realize that their opinions, backed at times with poor post-prandial jests, are powerless to damage the reputation of a man, whose works have been performed with success for a century and have been approved by many highly competent judges. As Sydney Smith advised in one of his essays, if one yearns to persecute some religious body, why not choose some small sect such as the Society of Friends rather than a powerful organization like the Roman Catholic Church. Cannot the foes of Berlioz grasp the simple fact that their abuse of him is in itself a testimony to his greatness? A lesser man would not excite their angry passions in the same way.

Berlioz's position as a musician would probably have been more secure if he had never published his Memoirs. Thanks to his picturesque prose and his literary talents, the man is better known than the artist. In some cases the music-lover ignores a composer's life, when judging his music; in others, he endows the musician with angelic and often purely imaginary attributes, on the principle that 'he who drives fat oxen should himself be fat'. Unconsciously or consciously, many of us do the contrary as regards Berlioz, and judge the oxen from what we believe the man to have been. In notices of Wagner's works one seldom, if ever, finds references to his private life: those of Berlioz, be they favourable or the reverse, constantly contain such references. And this illogical confusion between the man and the artist is another instance of the unfair treatment accorded the French composer. If we elect to picture a scatter-brained young man, infatuated by a theatrical star, incorrigibly lazy over his studies, and a deliberate, if polished, liar, we are naturally disposed to find in his music insincerity and errors of technique. I would emphasize the 'young man', because I believe that few picture him as a man in middle life, prematurely aged by disappointment and by bouts of agonizing pain, courageously fighting till the end.

As regards the nomenclature of the works I may appear to have been inconsistent. At times I have used the French title, at others the English one. The latter I have usually employed, when there is a generally accepted name, or when the French one can be translated literally. In other cases I have preferred the original title, as less open to misunderstanding.

I would here acknowledge my indebtedness to Mr. Ernest Newman, who has written on Berlioz at greater length and with fuller understanding than any other English writer. My warm thanks are due to my friends W. F. H. Blandford, Hubert W. Farren, and Jacques Barzun. To the first for undertaking the ungrateful task of correcting the proofs and compiling an index; to the second for drawing my attention to many references to Berlioz which would otherwise have escaped my attention; to the third for having consulted on my behalf many of Berlioz's scores (annotated by the composer) which are now in the Bibliothèque Nationale in Paris.

The bibliography makes no pretence of being complete, since it only includes works in my own library.

TOM S. WOTTON

Hastings, 1934.

CONTENTS

Chapter One

INTRODUCTORY

THE wish to know something of the life and character of a great man is a natural one. Whether, in the case of an artist, this knowledge will help us to understand his works is problematical. So many instances might be adduced of extraordinary divergences between the man and the artist, that it would seem that there is some niche, some sanctuary, in the brain of a genius that is entirely independent of external influences, and is unexplained by any theory of heredity. As Berlioz said,[1] 'There is within me an inexplicable mechanism which functions in spite of reason, and I allow it to function, because I cannot prevent it.' Taking this to be generally true, we must not forget that we are dependent on the man for the delivery of the message from the secret shrine. The voice of the god reaches us only through the mouth of his prophet, and hence some knowledge of the latter is of moment that we may have some means of estimating how much the divine message has suffered in transmission, as suffer it must, because the god is always greater than his prophet.

In the case of Hector Berlioz there are many who are inclined to doubt the existence of the god, since to them the prophet hesitates and stammers too much in his musical speech to warrant there being any inspiration. Others deny this hesitancy; or, admitting its occasional occurrence, declare that it does not detract from the truth or clarity of the message, nay, that it is often more effective than the precise diction so common with mediocrities.

He who listens to the message is also of importance; and one of his endeavours should be that of placing himself in the position of the original audience. It is

[1] *Correspondance inédite*, Letter LXXXIV.

B

not easy! What to the first hearers of Beethoven's symphonies were tricks of orchestration, calling forth the sarcasm of the youthful Weber, to-day are commonplaces. Even so magical an effect as that of the muted horns in the 'Tarnhelm' motive cannot move us as it did the pilgrims to Bayreuth in 1876. It has been the same in other ways, and thus of necessity we lose much of the force of the composer's thought. It is obvious that, if he expresses it by means of original orchestration and original harmony, the effect—as far as the present-day listener is concerned—is weakened when both the orchestration and the harmony have entered into everyday usage. Berlioz, however, has suffered comparatively little from a vulgarization of his medium of expression, since he has had no direct imitators, though we can trace his influence in many ways. Most of his ideas seem as fresh to-day as when they were minted.

Many listeners are perhaps inclined to look upon Berlioz as being a more modern composer than he was. It may be a compliment to him, but at the same time it is unfair, since, though he anticipated much that is to be found in modern music, we—maybe unconsciously—do not judge music composed in this present year of grace by quite the same standards as we apply to the works of the old masters. We must bear in mind the fact that Berlioz had finished his career before the later operas of Wagner were produced. And as his style, unlike that of the German master, remained unchanged throughout his life, only becoming more mature as he gained experience, we shall perhaps understand him better, if we regard him as being a composer of the 1830's, a decade which included the Fantastic Symphony in its revised form, the *Rob Roy* and *King Lear* Overtures, *The Fifth of May*, the *Requiem*, *Benvenuto Cellini*, and his Second, Third, and Fourth Symphonies, to say nothing of *Sara la baigneuse*, *Summer Nights*, and other minor works. As he wrote to

Adolphe Samuel after the production of *The Childhood of Christ*[1] in 1854, 'The good folk of Paris say that I have changed my style, that I have "improved". It is unnecessary to tell you that I have merely altered my subject.'

To understand the character of Berlioz the man, we may learn much from the opinions of his contemporaries, but as these are often coloured by the bias of the writer or speaker, it is well not to place too much stress on them. His own writings tell us a great deal more, though even with them we must use discrimination. To saddle him with the ideas expressed in some of his articles would be unfair. He was forced to write them to keep the wolf from his door, and to ensure their acceptance had to conform to the policy of the particular journal in which they appeared. His notice of *Le Prophète*,[2] for instance, by no means represents his real opinion of the opera, which, Saint-Saëns tells us, he loathed. But Meyerbeer was too powerful, and his music too firmly enshrined in the hearts of the Parisians for even the *Débats* to question its merits. On the whole, however, from his numerous articles we can gather a fairly faithful picture of the man, the musical creed to which he held unswervingly throughout his life, his likes and dislikes, his rather grim sense of humour, his poetic fancy, his proneness at times to exaggeration and to piling up his superlatives in the endeavour to express his feelings—in short, we are able to form a tolerably accurate idea of the character of the prophet who delivers the divine message. But we must be careful not to place undue emphasis on any single trait. Led astray by his occasional habit of exaggeration, many have found the same fault in nearly every score he penned, and, worse still, have thought

---

[1] Here and elsewhere I have used the accepted English title of the work, but I would point out that it is a mistranslation. The trilogy has nothing to do with the childhood of Christ.

[2] Included in *Les Musiciens et la musique*, Paris, 1903.

to do him a service by introducing exaggeration into the rendering of his works. As we shall see, in this respect at least, Berlioz the musician must not be judged by our estimate of Berlioz the man.

Of the four books published in his lifetime *Voyage musical en Allemagne et en Italie* (1844) is practically reproduced in his later literary works, with a few retouches that possess greater value for the psychologist than the musician. In *Les Grotesques de la musique* (1859) we find much of that grim humour to which I have alluded. Even in some of his music I would see something of the same quality. His own description of the Orgy of the *Harold in Italy* Symphony seems to bear out my idea. The two other books, *Les Soirées de l'orchestre* (1852) and *A travers chants* (1862), both consisting principally of articles and feuilletons already published, are of value, inasmuch as he was free to express his opinions untrammelled by the 'policy' of any journal.

Berlioz in his Memoirs tells us how he detested journalism. 'To write nothing about nothing! To deal out lukewarm praise and insufferable insipidities! To speak of a great master one day, and the next of a *crétin* with the same seriousness, in the same language! To devote one's time, one's intelligence, one's courage, one's patience to this task, with the certitude of not being of the slightest service to art.... Oh! It is the height of humiliation!' Nevertheless, he must have enjoyed carrying out some of his duties. He would have revelled in criticizing Gluck or Beethoven, and I do not fancy he experienced much difficulty in writing a column and a half in praise of the *Hebrides* Overture in *La Gazette musicale*.[1] Judging by the length and number of those of his letters that have

---

[1] I have particularly singled out the criticism of the overture, since one of the minor superstitions as regards Berlioz is that he did not appreciate the music of Mendelssohn. On the contrary, he was enthusiastic over the *Walpurgis Night* and the symphonies, and even applauded the two oratorios, although German sacred music did not as a rule appeal to him.

been preserved, he certainly had no objection to the physical exertion of writing. We were promised a complete collection of them some thirty years ago, but, like so many other promises relating to Berlioz and his works, it has never been carried out.[1] As it is, the letters are scattered through so many books and magazines that it is almost impossible for any one to be cognizant of all of them, and thus it is easy to overlook something of importance in estimating the character of our prophet. From a psychological point of view the letters to Berlioz's lifelong friend, Humbert Ferrand, are of immense value. To his own family—except perhaps to l is father in his earlier years and his sister Adèle in his later ones—the composer wrote perfunctorily, partly because of their want of sympathy with his chosen career and his selection of a wife, but perhaps principally because he knew that his letters would probably be read by a number of persons outside the family circle—in those days a letter from Paris was an event in a small village. To Ferrand alone he laid bare his soul. Unfortunately, since Ferrand was no musician, his friend only touched on the poetic side of his compositions. Had it been otherwise, we might have had more information as regards the origin of the Fantastic Symphony and other of his works. Whether these *Lettres intimes* are textually accurate and without omissions, I do not know, nor how far the collection is complete. The letters that Berlioz wrote from Italy, when he was contemplating the murder of his faithless fiancée, are not included, having been probably destroyed by Ferrand on their receipt; and others may

[1] Such a collection in order to possess any real value should naturally be without mutilation. It may seem superfluous to insist upon this point, but it is necessary. The *Correspondance inédite* does not appear to be always accurate, and in another collection of Berlioz's letters all technical details are omitted, thanks possibly to the publisher rather than the editor, but in any case an outrageous proceeding. The importance of these omissions may be judged by the fact hat in one letter, extracted from a more conscientious collection, the technical details refer to alterations in the Finale of the *Harold in Italy* Symphony not recorded in any edition of the score.

have shared the same fate. In spite of the strong friendship between the two men, they were sharply divided on one important point. While Ferrand was a devout Catholic, Berlioz was a free-thinker, and as such must often have shocked his friend as he shocked, rather with malice aforethought, Mendelssohn at Rome. It is strange that so many letters of a great man should be preserved. One would have thought that those who loved him would burke letters penned under great mental stress, when the writer was obviously not himself. In any case, it is spiteful to collate too closely those, written hurriedly under some strong emotion, with the man's public utterances. After all, by reading them we are doing something which, were the writer living, would be discreditable.

From a musical standpoint, the sixty-three letters of Berlioz in the three volumes of *Briefe an Franz Liszt* are the most valuable, since the latter was almost the only musician with whom the French composer was on terms of real intimacy. He of course discussed music in his letters to Hans von Bülow, Adolphe Samuel (twenty-six letters in *Le Ménestrel* of 1879), Morel, and others, but he was not on the same terms with them. Unfortunately, towards the end of his life Berlioz's friendship with Liszt was dimmed owing to the jealousy of Marie Recio, his second wife. Although Liszt had helped him with performances of his works at Weimar, he realized, what was undoubtedly the truth, that his friend's admiration for his music had been largely replaced by one for Wagner's compositions. And such disappointment as he not unnaturally experienced was aggravated by Marie's clacking tongue. It also affected his relations with Wagner, as the German master perfectly appreciated. Berlioz's correspondence with Liszt is partially completed by his letters to Princess Carolyne Sayn-Wittgenstein, which he hoped would be read also by Liszt. But this vicarious mode of communication was not the same as the direct one. Berlioz was flattered by the Princess's interest in his work, and her insistence—the idea possibly originating with Liszt—that he should write an opera based on Virgil's *Aeneid*, but I doubt whether he entertained any particular liking for the lady. The expansiveness of his letters is little more than that which he exhibits in his feuilletons and articles. And he touches rarely on the musical side of *The Trojans*.

Space forbids our dwelling on the character of our prophet so far as may be gathered from a study of his letters. They may be a truer guide than the Memoirs, but the latter demand more attention, since they are the best known of Berlioz's writings, and have invited the greatest amount of criticism, much of it swayed by a misconception (honest or the reverse) of the author's intentions, or by a desire of the critic to display the extent of his erudition and laborious research. To a lover of the master the continual harping on trivial inaccuracies, the dubbing the composer a deliberate liar on insufficient grounds, are distressing. The position of the critics would be stronger if they could support their case by the opinion of Berlioz's contemporaries of the truth of the Memoirs. But this they seldom, if ever, do. Yet out of the 500 pages of the first edition (published in 1870 in large 8vo) only 138 had not previously appeared in some form or another, certain episodes having been published as much as twenty-five years before. For example, the story of Habeneck taking (or being about to take) a pinch of snuff at one of the most important moments of the *Requiem* appeared in *Le Monde illustré* of 1859. At that date some hundreds of persons were living who had figured in either the chorus, or the orchestra, or the audience of the first performance, and were competent to deny or affirm the truth of the tale, which, as Berlioz told Ferrand in a letter of 28 April, 'created a sensation'. Probably Berlioz's pebble did not make so many ripples as he supposed, but nevertheless the story must have been discussed in musical circles. Yet Ernest Reyer, reviewing the Memoirs in the *Journal des débats* of 15 May 1871, accepted the tale as true, though he added that Habeneck's behaviour was 'probably not dictated by that evil intention attributed to it by Berlioz'. That the celebrated conductor was in the habit of taking snuff during performance seems to have been a fact, since M. Julien Tiersot made inquiries on this point amongst orchestral musicians who had played under Habeneck. As Berlioz was aware of this unfortunate habit, he must have been on the alert. The slightest movement of the conductor's hand in the direction of the pocket wherein reposed the *tabatière* would have aroused the composer's suspicions, and he would have acted as described in the Memoirs. He had good reason to be mistrustful of conductors after Grasset had ruined the final conflagration of *The Death of Sardanapalus*, and Girard had spoilt the effect of the first movement of the *Harold in Italy* Symphony from his inability to observe the tempo indications.

Hippeau[1] and Jullien[2] doubt Berlioz's story, basing their disbelief on the fact that he did not mention it at the time to his confidant, Humbert Ferrand. Musicians and writers on music may not be overburdened with a keen sense of logic, but nevertheless the two eminent critics I have cited might have had the wit to see the weakness of their argument—that, because Berlioz did not himself tell Ferrand, *therefore* the latter was not told. As a matter of fact, the composer did not write to his friend until twelve days after the performance of the *Requiem*—he was seldom so dilatory! —and commenced his letter, 'Flayol wrote to you some eight or ten days ago; for that reason I have waited....' What warranty have those who discredit the story of the snuff-box for asserting so positively that Flayol's letter did not contain full particulars of the incident,

---

[1] *Berlioz intime*, Paris, 1883.
[2] *Hector Berlioz, sa vie et ses œuvres*, Paris, 1888.

which, as Berlioz told Ferrand in 1859, appears in a 'much diluted' form in the Memoirs? M. Adolphe Boschot,[1] ever ready to brand Berlioz a liar with or without evidence, declares Berlioz's tale to be a figment of his brain, since, had it been true, there would have been some mention of it in the press, in which the composer would have 'screamed louder than all the trumpets of his Last Judgement'. Setting aside the fact that few editors would have been anxious to publish a scandal that involved a favourite conductor, a cabinet minister (Cavé), the venerable head of the Conservatoire, and goodness alone knows who else, the composer's friends would have advised him strongly against making a grievance out of what might have been merely inadvertence on the part of Habeneck. That this is what probably happened is borne out by an article by L. E.[2] in *Temple Bar* of October 1883. He relates how Berlioz asked the advice of himself and other friends whether he should include the tale of the snuff-box in his Memoirs. They unanimously vetoed any idea of telling it to the world. I take it that Berlioz's friends were equally unanimous a dozen years before. My position may not be impregnable, but I am better entrenched than those whose emphatic beliefs might be blown sky-high, if Flayol's letter ever came to light.

The Memoirs are of value, not only as an aid to forming our estimate of Berlioz's character, but because they contain a vast amount of information relative to musical conditions in France, Germany, Russia, and England during a large portion of the last century. All books of the autobiographical type contain inaccuracies, for the simple reason that no author has at hand the material that is subsequently collected by his commentators, even if he keeps an impossibly complete

[1] *Un Romantique sous Louis-Philippe*, Paris, 1908.
[2] Probably Louis Engel, at that time a well-known critic and musicologue resident in London.

diary from his earliest years. Impressions recorded at
the time in all honesty may not be in strict accord
with the absolute facts. Memoirs, to be of value, must
be viewed from the proper angle. In the case of those
of Berlioz it is imperative, because, should we omit
to do so, we are liable to form a wrong idea of the
musician. No prophet is honoured in his own country,
because his neighbours, knowing his frailties and
possibly not impressed by his personal appearance,
cannot believe him to be the transmitter of a divine
message. Many people, if it be dinned often enough
into their ears that Berlioz is a liar, will take it as
gospel, doubt the sincerity of the man, and discover
insincerity in his music.

M. Adolphe Boschot, Berlioz's most exhaustive,
and unfortunately most unsympathetic, biographer, is
obsessed with the conviction of the untruthfulness of
the composer. He may boast of having unearthed 'at
least one document' for each week of Berlioz's mature
life. But, as Dr. Jacques Barzun[1] observes:—

'The use he has made of these tons of paper is unfortunately
of little worth, for he fails constantly to keep in mind the
numerical and spiritual ratio between the acts of life and the
documents that record them. A man, and especially a man of
the most inexhaustible genius like Berlioz, lives in at least two
planes, one of prosaic activity and a second of fertile creative-
ness and the importance of each to the genius himself is not to
be estimated by balancing laundry bills against symphonies.
But M. Boschot is so impressed by the "testimony" of scraps
of paper that he forgets why he has collected them, namely to
understand Berlioz.'

To attempt to write on Berlioz without consulting
documents and previous authorities would be an im-
pertinence. But more harm is done by the misuse of
authorities, by taking negative evidence to be absolute
proof—a common fault of illogical minds—or by

[1] 'The "New" Biography, or *de* Mortuis Nil Nisi Bunkum' (*The Lion
and Crown*, 1933).

accepting as witnesses for the prosecution those whose reliability is suspect. For examples of the first I may refer the reader to many examples to be found in M. Boschot's three volumes: as an instance of the second method, I would cite the much more understanding and sympathetic Edmond Hippeau. The latter relies largely, especially with respect to Berlioz's matrimonial difficulties, on Ernest Legouvé, the celebrated playwright, whose *Soixante ans de souvenirs* contains a chapter devoted to the composer. I must confess that I have not read the whole book, but I have no reason to think that Legouvé's memory is more treacherous than that of other writers of souvenirs. In this particular chapter, however, he relates how Berlioz dragged himself from a sick-bed to vote for Charles Blanc (at whose hands he had received a kindness twenty years before) who was seeking election to the Academy. 'A fortnight later he [Berlioz] was dead' concludes Legouvé—Hippeau, by the way, reducing the interval to a week. Now, the election took place on 25 November 1868, and Berlioz did not die till the following March! I would not place too much stress on Legouvé's *lapsus calami*—as a dramatist, he was tempted to conclude his story dramatically— but if Berlioz had been guilty of such a slip, how the gadflies would have fastened on it! I would merely observe that, if I found a witness so unreliable as regards events that had occurred only a few years before he recorded them, I should be extremely cautious in accepting his testimony in respect of those of thirty or forty years before.

As Berlioz said in his preface to *The Damnation of Faust*, 'possibly these remarks may seem puerile to those nimble wits (*excellents esprits*) who are wont to see at once into the *heart* of things', but, unhappily, in writing of the French master, before one can obtain a clear view of the picture, it must be cleansed from accumulated grime. I repeat, that there are no

more inaccuracies in Berlioz's Memoirs than there are
in the majority of such books. As the level-headed
Romain Rolland says, 'The errors of the Memoirs
have been much exaggerated. And besides, Berlioz
was the first to point out, in his preface, that "he would
only tell what it pleased him to tell", and that "he was
not writing his *Confessions* [in the style of J. J. Rous-
seau]". Who would dream of reproaching him for this?'[1]
Even in passages where his memory was most at fault,
it is often easy to understand how it betrayed him. In
Harmonie et mélodie Saint-Saëns says,

'It is because he [Berlioz] took himself to be a Faust, a
Manfred, that he has depicted himself in his Memoirs in very
false colours, pretending to hate mankind, he who the smallest
mark of sympathy moved to tears. He only hated the *profanum
vulgus*, like Horace, like all artists and all poets. In reality, he
was not only sincere, he was naïve in the best sense, naïve like
Haydn, at whose naïvety he was so ready to laugh.'

The opening words of the above I venture to question.
Berlioz did not try deliberately to mould himself on
Faust, Manfred, or René. He was the character itself
in some respects, and hence his admiration for the
plays of Goethe and Shakespeare and the tales of
Chateaubriand, finding therein some image of himself.

Berlioz was almost the only composer of any note
who can be considered as a child of the Revolution,
the official date of his birth being 19 Frimaire of the
year XII of the Republic (9 December 1803). He
belonged to a generation whose ideas and feelings are
difficult for us to understand, although they were somewhat analogous to those engendered by the Great War.
For many years, with the opening year of the last
century as centre, all Europe was (as now) in a state
of unrest. New ideas in science, in art, in religion, in
the destinies of humanity, had permeated all the western
nations and every section of society. In France, where

---

[1] 'Berlioz', *La Revue de Paris*, 1 March 1904.

those ideas had been transformed into deeds, the effect of them was considerably greater. As regards the mass of the population, the glitter and military pomp of the first Empire did much to change the current of their thoughts. But there still remained a large number of intellectual men, more especially amongst those cursed with the artistic temperament, with minds still torn by doubts and longings for they knew not what. This *mal du siècle* in Berlioz's case may have been aggravated by heredity. His father, Dr. Berlioz, appears to have led a tranquil, philosophical life, but the large doses of opium he was compelled to take to assuage his agonizing intestinal pains could scarcely have fitted him to be an ideal parent from the eugenic point of view. We find the 'malady of the century' described in Chateaubriand's works, in Alfred de Musset's *Confessions d'un enfant du siècle*, and can gather some idea of it from passages scattered throughout Berlioz's own writings. For instance, he prefaces his account of his aimless wanderings in Paris and the environs after seeing *Hamlet* in September 1827:

'The shock was too great, and I was long in recovering. To an intense, profound mental disturbance, impossible to surmount, was joined a nervous, not to say pathological, condition of which a clever psychologist alone could give an appropriate idea.'

Early in January 1830 he appears to have had a recurrence of the same symptoms, aggravated by toothache. On this occasion his emotions found relief in the composition of his *Elegy*, and I suspect that at other times music served him as a safety-valve.

Quite apart, however, from this mysterious *mal du siècle*, the sudden change from the uneventful life of his village to the turmoil of Paris must have had an enormous effect on one so highly strung as himself. To a 'shy and ignorant youngster', such he declares himself to have been during his first years in the capital, with a countryman's mistrust of the townsfolk, the effort required to obtain recognition and to bring himself to the notice of all and sundry must have been a constant strain, as every one afflicted with shyness will realize. At times it led him to commit audacities from which a more sophisticated person might recoil. The Memoirs touch lightly on his medical studies, but, until he finally discarded them on his entrance into the Conservatoire in 1826, he must have worked at them, if only half-heartedly. Two years after his arrival in Paris in November 1821, he was admitted as *bachelier ès sciences physiques*. At the same time he was endeavouring to atone for his lack of musical training, and striving to express himself in a language he as yet understood imperfectly. There is no need to dwell on the privations he underwent. Probably at the time he paid little heed to them, though no doubt he suffered from their effects later. During his early years in Paris his brain must have been working at abnormal pressure, and that he did not collapse, mentally and physically, is a matter of surprise. As we shall see in our next chapter, probably he was saved by Camille Moke from what we should call nowadays a 'nervous breakdown'.

Berlioz's failure to obtain the *Prix de Rome* in 1828 with his cantata *Herminia* must have affected him deeply, though he himself in the Memoirs is inclined to jest on the matter. As M. Tiersot says,[1]

'It is incomprehensible why this cantata was not considered worthy of the first prize. It is well written, and displays technical qualities which are lacking in some notable composers of the time. As to imagination, there is more in its hundred pages of orchestral score than in all the cantatas submitted for ten years and after! It is moreover restrained, clear, and well balanced, which shows that Berlioz took great pains and, when penning it, constantly thought of the judges whose suffrages he sought.'

[1] *Le Ménestrel* of 2 Sept. 1906, in one of the instalments of *Berlioziana* which ran through the journal for many months.

The alleged reason for the examiners' attitude was that Berlioz, perfectly justified by the words of the poem, had set four lines as a prayer (Largo) instead of including them in the final aria (Allegro). It is of interest to note that this crime apparently did not seem so heinous to the non-musical members amongst the examiners—the painters, writers, architects. At the first vote, when only musicians were present, Berlioz was not even accorded a place. At the second vote, with a mixed jury, he was awarded a second prize. The Philistines evidently could not appreciate the enormity of failing to set words commencing 'God of the Christians' as an 'aria di bravura'. A pupil of Cherubini's, Guillaume Ross-Despréaux, who may have died young, but certainly never did anything to vindicate the examiners' decision, secured the first prize. Berlioz of course must have realized to the full the gross injustice of the treatment meted out to him ; and those who object to his divergences from academic usage should remember that from the beginning its supporters gave him small cause to admire it.

It is tempting to wonder what would have happened if his cantata had been accepted, and he had been sent to Italy in 1828 instead of two years later. As far as his life was concerned, he probably would have been happier. It is reasonable to suppose that he would have forgotten his infatuation for Harriet Smithson. He would not have met Camille Moke, who, whatever temporary blessings she may have bestowed, embittered his life later by her heartless behaviour. The Fantastic Symphony would never have been written, though probably some of its music would have appeared in another guise. Instead, we should have had a 'Faust' Symphony, such as he had originally contemplated. Perhaps the principal difference his earlier departure for Italy might have made would have been as regards his reputation in Paris. Remembered as the composer of the innocuous *Herminia* he would

have found many doors open to him that were closed
to the composer of the revolutionary Fantastic Symphony. To be chained to the benches of the Conservatoire for two years as a student, when he felt himself
(rightly or wrongly) to be a greater man than his
masters, must have tried him sorely. How a sojourn
in Germany, which in the normal course should have
followed his time in Rome, would have affected him
is problematical. Dependent on the town to which he
was sent, from what we know of musical conditions
in Germany in 1830, they might have disgusted him
as much as those in Italy.

Amongst the Romantics of France, few could have
possessed the hypersensitiveness of Berlioz. Even
amongst musicians, who are possibly more highly
strung than other artists, it would be difficult in this
respect to find his equal. As illustrative of this sensi-
tiveness, take his description of the effect the hearing
of music produced on him. As his account appears in
the first article of *A travers chants* (1862), and as this is
a partial reproduction of one of his earliest essays,[1]
evidently his abnormal response to music persisted
throughout his life, though it was naturally more
intense when he was a young man.

‘On hearing certain pieces of music my vital forces seem at
first to be doubled. I feel a delicious pleasure, in which intelligence plays no part; the habit of analysis then asserts itself
and gives birth to admiration; an emotion increasing propor-
tionately to the energy or grandeur of the composer’s concep-
tions soon produces a strange effect on my circulation; my
arteries pulsate violently; tears, which as a rule announce the
end of the paroxysm, often indicate only a progressive stage
soon to be passed. In this case, there follow spasmodic contractions of the muscles, trembling of the limbs, *a total absence of
sensation in hands and feet*, a partial paralysis of the visual and
auditory nerves. I no longer see, I hardly hear! Giddiness
. . . semi-unconsciousness.’

[1] ‘Aperçu sur la musique dramatique et la musique romantique’, *Le
Correspondant*, 22 Oct. 1830.

By music he dislikes he is equally moved:

'I crimson as with shame, and am filled with absolute indignation; to see me one would believe that I had been the
recipient of some unpardonable insult. To be quit of the impression, there is a general upheaval, an effort of excretion
throughout the organism, analogous to attempts to vomit, when
the stomach would rid itself of some nauseating liquid. It is
disgust and hate carried to their extreme limits; this music
exacerbates me and I vomit it through all my pores.'

We may discount something for the anxiety of the
ex-medical student to give a correct diagnosis, and
something perhaps for the tendency of a literary man
towards exaggeration, but what remains is no doubt a
true description of the extraordinary effect music produced on him. It is corroborated by many passages
in his letters. And one marvels how he managed to
retain sufficient command of himself to permit him to
conduct, especially his own works, which, as with
every other composer, affected him most strongly. On
several occasions he seems to have been on the verge
of a break-down at performance, and to have been
saved from mishap by the exercise of that indomitable
will that he undoubtedly possessed. He could not
have accomplished so much as he did had he lacked it.

This temperamental hypersensitiveness was, however, not without its compensations. It was correlated
with an abnormal sense of hearing and an appreciation
of shades of tone-colour which grosser ears would be
unable to detect. As without question he *felt* music in
a way that few, if any, had before him, he was able
to strike new notes in it. Imitative music was almost
coeval with music itself; but that 'atmosphere', for
which painters strove, was seldom present in the sister
art. The mysterious nocturnal feeling of the opening
chords of the distant chorus that prefaces the Love
Scene of the *Romeo and Juliet* Symphony was a new
experience in music. We can find similar passages elsewhere in the composer's scores; and it must be added

that, though something may be due to the orchestration, often very discreet, much depends on the harmony. Here and there we find a curious suggestion of space, and it is not difficult to discover in his music sentiments hitherto unexpressed.

Above I have said that Liszt was almost the only musician with whom Berlioz was on terms of real intimacy. But probably the one who knew him best was Saint-Saëns, and for that reason I have relied largely on him in my estimate of the subject of this book. Berlioz and Liszt met for the first time the day before the first performance of the Fantastic Symphony, and conceived a deep sympathy for one another. The ten years' difference in their ages counted for little. The pianist, already a celebrity, was a man of the world, while Berlioz, unknown beyond a small circle, had still much of the provincial clinging to him. It would be a commonplace to add, that an intimacy begun in one's early years must always hold something which a later friendship can never possess. Saint-Saëns's first meeting with Berlioz was in December 1853, when the first symphony of the former was produced anonymously. Soon after he was entrusted with the piano arrangement of *Lélio*, and becoming a personal friend of its author, with the keen sight of gifted youth discovered the real man, whom the world deemed to be 'haughty, spiteful, and evil. On the contrary he was good, good to the verge of weakness, grateful for the slightest marks of interest evinced in him, and of an admirable simplicity that enhanced his sallies and mordant wit, since one never felt that he was striving after effect nor that desire to astonish his audience which spoils so many good things.'[1] The thirty-two years' difference in the ages of the two composers may have prevented such an intimacy as existed between Berlioz and Liszt, but not materially. Berlioz's was a very transparent nature, and when the two were

[1] *Portraits et souvenirs.*

in Paris Saint-Saëns must have come across him almost daily. The capital in those days was not a large place. Although the picture drawn by Saint-Saëns differs largely from the generally accepted one, I take it to be correct. Admiration and sincere affection may have softened his portrait, but even that is doubtful. Since he was cast in a different mould, I question whether he altogether approved Berlioz's goodness, his naïvety, or his simplicity. When he exclaimed 'Why should anyone wish to deceive him, he who deceived no one ?', apropos of Berlioz's touching belief in the promises that were made him by those who had no intention of fulfilling them, I fancy there was a trace of pity for this persistent faith. 'He who deceived no one !' It is difficult to realize that this is the Machiavellian creature of the legend, who cunningly scattered deliberate lies throughout the pages of his Memoirs, and was such a blind fool as to include many that told against him. The only chapter in which he deliberately veiled the truth is that dealing with his relations with Camille Moke. It is not a matter of surprise ! Few men would be disposed to discuss at length their entanglement with a girl, who was indubitably a shameless flirt.[1] But mark the guilelessness of the man ! A few chapters farther on he relates the *Drame* (he calls it *Épisode bouffon* in *Voyage musical*) of his setting forth from Italy to slay a young woman, who is obviously the object of the 'violent distraction' of the previous one. We must not forget that when the *Épisode bouffon* appeared in 1844, there was no necessity for Berlioz to dot all his i's. All Paris knew of the composer's engagement to Mlle Moke, and of

[1] Four years after her marriage to Pleyel she left the house one evening in company with a young man, with whom she undoubtedly passed the night, returning the next morning in a battered condition which argued an encounter with some jealous rival. Pleyel forgave her, and to repay his generosity, she left home for good some few days later. The husband obtained from the Courts a separation *de corps et de biens*. (See *La Gazette des Tribunaux*, quoted by Boschot in *Une Vie romantique*.)

her jilting him for Pleyel. Berlioz deceived nobody.
When he included the tale in his Memoirs, he added
a footnote to the effect that the mother of his 'amiable consolatrix' announced the marriage of her
daughter to M. P——. Knowing the whole truth, it is
difficult to estimate how much a reader of the present
day would gather from that footnote. Is it far-fetched
to imagine that Berlioz, who ' was noi writing his confessions', believed that his hint would be sufficient for
future generations? Even amongst musicians it is unusual for a man to contemplate the murder of a girl
simply because she intends to wed some one else,
unless he is strongly convinced that he has a prior
claim on her affections.

If we bear in mind Saint-Saëns's portrait of Berlioz
—and I see no reason for doubting its truthfulness—
I believe we shall find corroboration in his letters and
Memoirs, though in the latter, as Saint-Saëns suggests,
he may in some respects have attempted to assume a
character that was not natural to him. Or rather, he
had assumed it so often, that it had become a second
nature to him. Like many shy people he donned a
defensive armour in face of the world. The accusation
of 'pushfulness' has been brought against him, but, if
I read him right, the imperative necessity for it distressed him quite as much as it appears to distress
some of his detractors. How else was he to obtain
recognition? Thanks to his family connexions, he had
the ear of a few high-placed men in Paris, such as the
Vicomte de la Rochefoucauld, but, if he had relied on
them, his scores might have lain forgotten, like those
of Bach and Schubert, awaiting some Mendelssohn,
some George Grove, to bring them to light. As the
tale goes, the youthful Nelson was taunted by his
shipmates before some engagement, because his knees
were trembling. The future admiral asserted (somewhat grandiloquently) that his body was aquake at
the thoughts of the deeds of daring it would be called

upon to perform. In Berlioz's case, there was a similar conflict 'twixt mind and temperament. When he had that long conversation with Wagner in London in 1855 —the only time when the two composers approached a mutual understanding—the German master was particularly impressed by the intense loneliness of his French colleague.

This terrible feeling of isolation, the *mal de l'isolement*, as Berlioz himself calls it, oppressed him all his life and accounts for many things. It explains his expansiveness, his eager desire to get into touch with some kindred spirit: it explains that tendency to be suspicious of others, noted by Reyer, and his rigid determination to plough his own furrow, mistrustful of developments, even when they were the logical evolution of his own theories; and it explains the shyness which, in spite of accepted ideas, I fancy was part and parcel of him. Some of his fellow students at the Villa Medici were inclined to regard him as somewhat of a *poseur*, and probably some of his behaviour, such as using a skull as a drinking-cup *à la Byron*, may have encouraged their belief. He himself would certainly have resented the imputation. He dreaded the household knowing that he at times passed his nights in the garden, lest he should be accused of 'swank' (*manière*). He had his little vanities, as, for instance, cultivating that extraordinary mop of hair, but few of us are exempt from them, and artists as a race seem peculiarly prone to them. Many of his poses were natural to him. As I have suggested, there was much of a Manfred, a René, inherent in him, and his solitary boyhood accentuated his natural bent. His very real love for Estelle, aggravated by its hopelessness, must have led to unhealthy brooding and introspection. Somewhere he admits that he was not a particularly pleasant companion during his early days in Rome, and we can understand his attitude. He had no wish to go to Italy, and was disgusted at the musical conditions he found there, to say nothing of his continual worry at not receiving letters from his fiancée, to whom he was undoubtedly strongly attached. Mendelssohn declared that his French acquaintance thought of nothing else but getting married, and we can imagine how bored he must have been at descriptions of Camille's charms. In any case, a shy lonely man, averse from society, is often credited with behaviour foreign to his real nature. That he felt a restraint in general society we know from some of his home letters, in which he touches on it as though his family were fully aware of his feelings.

Berlioz's 'pushfulness' was forced upon him; his anxiety to obtain some settled post—conductor at the Opéra, a professorship at the Conservatoire, and the like—was prompted by a desire to possess a fixed income in order that he might have opportunities for composing free from the eternal grind of writing press-notices. His 'poses' were ingrained in him. If he had completed his medical studies, and led the hum-drum life of a country doctor, he probably would have had much the same reputation. Where he exhibited any deliberation in connexion with his poses—and after all, its deliberateness is surely one of the essentials of a pose—was in using them as a means of advertising himself and bringing himself to the notice of the public, impelled by the far from ignoble wish to obtain recognition as a musician. We shall find an example of this in the next chapter. I would only remark here that, in so doing, he often displayed great naïvety, as great as that of many a modern writer (male or female), who innocently believes that a portrait in the newspapers will induce the public to purchase his or her books. In Paris a hundred years ago, when all the world knew of the relations of George Sand with Alfred de Musset, Chopin, and others, and of Liszt with the Comtesse d'Agoult, the infatuation of Berlioz for Harriet Smithson must have seemed rather a tame affair, decidedly lacking in spice.

In estimating the character of our prophet we must not leave out of account one weakness, probably due to his race. The Dauphinois seem to be rather given to treasuring up both kindnesses and wrongs, and to possess a determination to 'get even' with the author of them. We have seen how Berlioz remembered a kindness after twenty years, and endeavoured to return it at great cost to himself. On the other hand, we have several examples of his 'petty vengeances', as he calls them, which, he explained to Hiller, 'were superfluous, but necessary'. Sometimes, as with respect to Cherubini, his 'getting his own back' was tinged by the schoolboyishness that he never outgrew. At times, however, his vengeances were undignified and unworthy of him, as when he introduced Camille Moke into two of his tales. They are one of the indices to his character. And we must not forget, although he was inclined to repudiate the idea in a letter to Ferrand, that we owe the Fantastic Symphony to this trait.

Chapter Two

THE LEGEND

AROUND every great man legends cluster. Some arise in spite of him; others he does not trouble to dissipate; some he may even encourage. Berlioz was no exception to the rule, and hence was responsible, directly or indirectly, for some of the opinions of himself and his music, which were prevalent during his lifetime and have persisted until the present day. The idea, for instance, that the major portion of his music is 'eccentric'. Nowadays, this may be mainly due to the fondness of the ordinary person for outworn clichés. But some of it originated with Berlioz. At the commencement of his career he believed that by drawing attention to himself he would arouse in the Parisians a desire to hear his music. In this he succeeded, but the result was not quite what he anticipated. As has been suggested in the last chapter, his 'poses' were genuine enough; but if his fellow students in Italy, who knew the manners and customs of the Bohemians depicted in Henry Murger's *Scènes de la vie de Bohème*, were inclined to deem him a *poseur*, we may be sure that the good bourgeois of Paris looked upon him as highly eccentric, and applied the same epithet to his music, since it is an undoubted truth that, when any one obtains a reputation for possessing any particular characteristic, many will detect it where it does not exist. Let a man once gain a reputation for wit, and his most fatuous remarks will be quoted as unquestionable proofs of it. That Berlioz soon after his arrival in Paris should have joined the ranks of the Romantics was but natural. He found amongst them kindred spirits. This alone would have made him suspect in the eyes of the Parisians. They would be apt to view his music with the same mistrust that they extended to the work of the Romantics in other directions.

What kind of music would the ordinary concert-goer of 1832—or, for a matter of that, of 1932—expect from the pen of a man described in the following terms?

'On the days when the English were not playing [that is, Kemble's company, of which Harriet Smithson was a member] Berlioz could not contemplate the idea of seeing Miss —— on the morrow without a shudder. He dreaded the moment as one of crisis or paroxysm! Then he might be found in a corner of the orchestra at the Odéon, pale, disordered and wild-eyed, his long hair and beard unkempt, listening, gloomy and taciturn, to some comedy of Picard's, which at times would wrench from him a terrible burst of hilarity, like that involuntary and miserable laughter resulting from the spasmodic contractions of the muscles in titillation. Pitied by some, he was an object of raillery for others. Humorists called him *Père la Joie.*'

This occurs in a notice in the *Revue de Paris* for December 1832 of the Fantastic Symphony, which was performed on the 9th of the month in its revised version, soon after the composer's return from Italy. The notice included a sketch of Berlioz's life, which, although ostensibly writtten by Joseph d' Ortigue (who included it in his *Le Balcon de l'opéra*), was practically penned by Berlioz himself. The late Charles Malherbe, in an article in the *Rivista musicale italiana* for 1906, relates how some manuscript notes of Berlioz were discovered at the Conservatoire—his first attempt at an autobiography—which had been utilized by d'Ortigue. Much of the two versions is collated, and the above paragraph, like many another, is practically the same in both cases, the published one varying, where the more practised pen of the journalist dictated the amelioration of some word or phrase. It will be noticed how the ex-medical student betrays himself. 'Crisis' and 'paroxysm' are used in a pathological sense, and the description of the laughter suggests a doctor's diagnosis.

As Berlioz had been recently introduced to Harriet and was recovering his past infatuation, his account of his love-lorn behaviour may have been intended primarily to induce that pity in her that is akin to love. But he also wanted to reawaken the interest of the public in himself and in his symphony, which was to be played again on 30 December. Unblushing advertisement? Possibly. But, as I suggested in the previous chapter, neither more nor less blatant than the self-advertisement of the present day, often without the excuse of trying to persuade a reluctant public to purchase one's artistic wares. Because he naïvely presented an unflattering picture of himself to arouse the interest of prospective concert-goers, it does not follow that his emotions at the Odéon and elsewhere were any the less real. They were perfectly genuine, with the possible reservation that we all have a tendency to exaggerate the outward and visible indications of our troubles when under the gaze of the public. There is nothing peculiar in his being able to record the spectacle he presented to others, as though, so to speak, he had been seated in the stalls and viewed his own performance on the stage. It is part of an artist's make-up, the power to observe almost dispassionately his own reactions to various emotions. What I am inclined to doubt is whether Berlioz's behaviour is to be attributed so much to his love for Harriet as he would have us believe, and as he had probably persuaded himself. The easiest person to deceive is oneself, and both sexes (perhaps more particularly the male) are apt to impute all their ills to the conduct of one of the opposite sex, though it must be admitted that many a man has been so far consistent as to attribute his successes to some feather-brained doll without two ideas in her head.

Harriet Smithson and Marie Recio were the two

in Paris Saint-Saëns must have come across him almost daily. The capital in those days was not a large place. Although the picture drawn by Saint-Saëns differs largely from the generally accepted one, I take it to be correct. Admiration and sincere affection may have softened his portrait, but even that is doubtful. Since he was cast in a different mould, I question whether he altogether approved Berlioz's goodness, his naïvety, or his simplicity. When he exclaimed 'Why should anyone wish to deceive him, he who deceived no one ?', apropos of Berlioz's touching belief in the promises that were made him by those who had no intention of fulfilling them, I fancy there was a trace of pity for this persistent faith. 'He who deceived no one !' It is difficult to realize that this is the Machiavellian creature of the legend, who cunningly scattered deliberate lies throughout the pages of his Memoirs, and was such a blind fool as to include many that told against him. The only chapter in which he deliberately veiled the truth is that dealing with his relations with Camille Moke. It is not a matter of surprise ! Few men would be disposed to discuss at length their entanglement with a girl, who was indubitably a shameless flirt.[1] But mark the guilelessness of the man ! A few chapters farther on he relates the *Drame* (he calls it *Épisode bouffon* in *Voyage musical*) of his setting forth from Italy to slay a young woman, who is obviously the object of the ' violent distraction ' of the previous one. We must not forget that when the *Épisode bouffon* appeared in 1844, there was no necessity for Berlioz to dot all his i's. All Paris knew of the composer's engagement to Mlle Moke, and of

[1] Four years after her marriage to Pleyel she left the house one evening in company with a young man, with whom she undoubtedly passed the night, returning the next morning in a battered condition which argued an encounter with some jealous rival. Pleyel forgave her, and to repay his generosity, she left home for good some few days later. The husband obtained from the Courts a separation *de corps et de biens*. (See *La Gazette des Tribunaux*, quoted by Boschot in *Une Vie romantique*.)

her jilting him for Pleyel. Berlioz deceived nobody.
When he included the tale in his Memoirs, he added
a footnote to the effect that the mother of his 'amiable consolatrix' announced the marriage of her
daughter to M. P——. Knowing the whole truth, it is
difficult to estimate how much a reader of the present
day would gather from that footnote. Is it far-fetched
to imagine that Berlioz, who ' was not writing his confessions', believed that his hint would be sufficient for
future generations? Even amongst musicians it is unusual for a man to contemplate the murder of a girl
simply because she intends to wed some one else,
unless he is strongly convinced that he has a prior
claim on her affections.

If we bear in mind Saint-Saëns's portrait of Berlioz
—and I see no reason for doubting its truthfulness—
I believe we shall find corroboration in his letters and
Memoirs, though in the latter, as Saint-Saëns suggests,
he may in some respects have attempted to assume a
character that was not natural to him. Or rather, he
had assumed it so often, that it had become a second
nature to him. Like many shy people he donned a
defensive armour in face of the world. The accusation
of 'pushfulness' has been brought against him, but, if
I read him right, the imperative necessity for it dis-
stressed him quite as much as it appears to distress
some of his detractors. How else was he to obtain
recognition? Thanks to his family connexions, he had
the ear of a few high-placed men in Paris, such as the
Vicomte de la Rochefoucauld, but, if he had relied on
them, his scores might have lain forgotten, like those
of Bach and Schubert, awaiting some Mendelssohn,
some George Grove, to bring them to light. As the
tale goes, the youthful Nelson was taunted by his
shipmates before some engagement, because his knees
were trembling. The future admiral asserted (somewhat grandiloquently) that his body was aquake at
the thoughts of the deeds of daring it would be called

women who, from the material point of view, most
affected Berlioz's life. But, from the spiritual point of
view, their influence was not to be compared with
that of Estelle Dubœuf and Camille Moke. Of the
reality of his boyish love for the former there can be
no doubt. His early adoration affected his character
in that it aggravated his *mal de l'isolement*; and without
question it also affected his music. She inspired some
of his melodies, and the chasteness of his love-music
owes much to the purity of his affection for the lady
of the *petits brodequins roses*. As Berlioz, without being
a sensualist, was not without experience of the grosser
manifestations of the sexual passion, one wonders what
would have been the result had he elected to paint
them. He, however, deliberately avoids the opportunity of so doing. He prefers to illustrate the balcony
scene in *Romeo and Juliet* rather than the subsequent
one in the heroine's chamber. In *The Damnation of
Faust* Faust's wooing is interrupted by Mephistopheles just as it begins to be interesting, as some
critic has cynically remarked. In the Royal Hunt of
The Trojans, when Aeneas and Dido enter the cave in
which she forgets her vows, there is no indication of
what is happening. And the beautiful love-duet of the
next act bears no traces of earthly passion.[1]

Taking Berlioz's love for Estelle as being a sacred
one, we may regard his love for Camille as his first
profane one. It is a matter for wonder that he mentioned her in his Memoirs. Her presence is explained
principally by the fact that he had related the *Épisode
bouffon* in his *Voyage musical*, published only three or
four years before he commenced his Memoirs. He
gave the episode in the earlier book because his strong
sense of humour prompted him to tell a good story
even though it were somewhat against himself, and

[1] On account of this absence of passion, in some performances of the
opera the Hunt is given *after* the duet. There is not the slightest warranty
for this in Berlioz's score.

possibly he wanted to give his own version of his departure from and return to Rome. In both the *Voyage* and the Memoirs he tells us that his comrades at the Villa Medici refrained from questioning him on what he had done, and he would have been loth to enlighten them. If he concealed the harmless fact of sleeping in the garden, lest his fellow students should consider it 'swank', he certainly would not have been anxious to endure their banter if he had described his projected disguise in feminine garments. But they must have discussed Berlioz's absence, and when later they learnt of Camille's marriage to Pleyel, there must have been much rumour about what the jilted lover had actually done. It was necessary that he should give his own account of his mad escapade.

When the composer first met Camille is uncertain. They were both teachers at the Institut Orthopédique directed by a Madame Daubrée, but the date of their joining the staff seems unknown. That, however, is immaterial. They would not have exchanged more than salutations when they met by chance, until Ferdinand Hiller asked Berlioz to convey his *billets-doux* to the young pianist. The German musician, in his *Künstlerleben*, gives his account of this, and no doubt it is substantially correct as regards the bare facts. But as his book was not published until 1880, fifty years after the meeting of Berlioz and Camille, he may well have forgotten details mentioned by the former which are dismissed by Hippeau as unlikely. Berlioz had much more reason for remembering the 'violent distraction'. This is Hiller's account:

'A young German musician [Hiller himself] had been received very graciously by a charming French colleague; they made music together under the eye of her mother, and so often and with such animation that they were anxious to see one another without mamma and without the piano. . . . My young compatriot had also made the acquaintance of Berlioz, who gave lessons on the guitar in a school where the former's *bien-aimée* was piano mistress. He had the naïvety to confide his love-affairs to Berlioz and beg him to act as love's messenger (*postillion d'amour*).'

Hippeau[1] comments on this: 'Here you see Berlioz guilty of an abuse of confidence as regards Hiller, guilty as regards Henrietta Smithson; Hiller deceived by both Camille and his friend.' Now, whatever may be thought of Berlioz's behaviour towards Hiller, how can he possibly have been guilty as regards Harriet? If Smith, Jones, or Robinson becomes infatuated with a film star, if he writes to her and receives no answer, if he seeks an introduction and is rebuffed, and if he eventually falls in love with some female acquaintance, surely no one would consider him in any way *guilty* as regards the star? For some inexplicable reason, however, Berlioz, even by some of his professed admirers, is judged by a standard totally opposed to that by which the rest of humanity is judged. Later on Hippeau remarks: 'His [Berlioz's] misadventure with Mlle Moke was in reality a very just punishment for his double betrayal of Miss Smithson and the excellent Hiller.' How in the name of wonder can a man betray in any sense of the word a woman to whom he has never spoken, and who refuses to have any dealings with him? A very just punishment! If a man is to be punished for every woman who is deaf to his entreaties, the lot of the average man would not be a happy one.

Strict moralists may not approve Berlioz's conduct as regards Hiller, but they should take into account the fact that the German was only a boy of seventeen, Camille being the same age. Doubtless a very nice boy, since Madame Moke (herself a German) seems to have given him the run of the house: yet still only a boy, whose attentions to her daughter she would not have taken seriously. I question whether Camille did. She was indubitably a shameless flirt, but, apart from

[1] *Berlioz intime.*

that, there is nothing extraordinary in a young girl discarding a boy of her own age in favour of a man ten years older, who was to boot already something of a celebrity. It is true that Berlioz should have been the last to undervalue the love of a boy. None of us, however, are disposed to admit that the troubles of others, from heart- to toothache, are quite so bad as our own. In any case I do not fancy that he had much choice in the matter. He was still in many ways the ' shy and ignorant youngster ', with no experience of women, and, if Camille in any degree resembled his subsequent description of her—and it was little exaggerated—he must have been as wax in her hands. Hippeau doubts whether Hiller (as reported by Berlioz) would have been so unwise as to say to Camille: 'Oh! I shall not be jealous of him! I am quite sure he will never love you!', and thus arouse in her the not unnatural curiosity to see whether this lover of the Irishwoman was really invulnerable. It becomes monotonous, this perpetual assumption that Berlioz was a liar! An experienced man of the world might not have made such a remark, cynically doubting whether Berlioz's infatuation was as great as he pretended or believed. With a boy of seventeen it would have been another matter. Unless human nature has altered considerably during the last hundred years, it was just the sort of chaff in which young people would indulge. It is, of course, only negative evidence, but in a letter from Hiller to Edmond Hippeau, dated Cologne 10/6/82,[1] he makes no attempt to contradict the account of the 'violent distraction' in the Memoirs. In the course of the letter he says:

'Filled by a certain idealism, which was scarcely apparent in my letters to Berlioz, I thought it honourable to remain the friend of the fiancé of her whom I imagined I adored. As to revenge, it was useless to attempt it. I am certain (with-

---

[1] Reproduced by Julien Tiersot in the *Rivista musicale italiana,* 1930, where the date is given as 10/6/32—obviously a printer's error.

out knowing it) that the marriage with Pleyel was already arranged when B. departed for Rome—I only gathered that from what every one said. Madame Moke certainly gasped "Ouf!" when she knew that her son-in-law (?) was out of France, and I do not fancy her daughter shed any tears. . . . . Our poor Berlioz was not happy in his relations with the *beau sexe*, but it must be confessed that it was his own fault.'

The first half of the last sentence is undoubtedly true: the second, however, is open to question. It *may* have been the fault of Berlioz that Camille preferred flirting with him rather than with Hiller. But he cannot be held responsible for her abominable conduct and that of her mother. If it had not been for Harriet's terrible jealousy, which, as we shall see, was probably largely without cause, and prevented his travelling abroad, he might have dwelt with her at least as contentedly as he did with Marie, whom he did not love as much.

Although I fail to understand how Berlioz could have in any way 'betrayed' Harriet, I fancy he did not transfer his affections to Camille without a struggle, if only because, having broadcast his admiration for the actress, he knew that the sudden extinguishing of it would excite ridicule. The attraction of Camille would no doubt have proved irresistible in any case; nevertheless he was anxious to have some reason for banishing Harriet from his thoughts. In a letter to Ferrand of 16 April 1830 he says that he has learned *affreuses vérités* concerning her, without specifying them or mentioning his informant. It may possibly have been Thomas Gounet, for in an undated letter to his friend[1] Berlioz writes: '*You have been, we have been* strangely deceived as regards H. S. . . .' Whether Gounet had

[1] *Lettres inédites de Hector Berlioz à Thomas Gounet*, with annotations by G. Allix, Grenoble, 1903. M. Allix suggests November 1832 as the date, but as Berlioz refers to the persecutions of his family (on account of his wishing to marry Harriet) it must be later. Prod'homme in the second edition of his *Hector Berlioz* (1927) gives it as April 1833, Tiersot as 7 Feb. (*Les années romantiques*).

really heard any scandal about Harriet, or had invented it—not a difficult thing to do with respect to an actress—with the kindly idea of dispelling Berlioz's absurd infatuation, is immaterial. Berlioz believed the scandal, because he wanted to believe it in order to justify his love for Camille, and in his heart of hearts he must have grown very tired of his sighings and whinings over this unapproachable goddess, who was frightened of him. These, however, are merely surmises. The point is, that Berlioz was very deeply in love with Camille. I should almost be inclined to term it the big love of his life, and this because it was a perfectly normal one and not mingled with other ideas or emotions. His love for Estelle, which, in a letter to Tajan-Rogé of 1 January 1848,[1] he singled out from his other loves, declaring that he 'still shuddered to think of it', most assuredly affected him enormously. But this devotion of a boy of twelve for a young woman six years his senior can scarcely be described as normal. Until Berlioz was introduced to Harriet at his concert of 9 December 1832, when the Fantastic Symphony was first given in its revised form, his infatuation for her was not the normal love of a man for a woman. In his letters to Ferrand, one has only to contrast those written when he called Harriet his Ophelia with those when Camille had him in thrall, to realize the fact. Although no doubt Berlioz deceived himself in the matter, his moanings and groanings in the former are very different from the healthy normal love expressed in the latter. Poets have sung of the beauty of love at first sight, and every lover has believed in the truth of it, forgetting the number of women by whom he was smitten at a distance, only to be woefully disappointed when he heard the lady's conversation. Even admitting that true love can be begotten through the medium of only one of our senses, I doubt whether it can exist for long without the co-

[1] *Le Musicien errant*, p. 211.

operation of the others, except for reasons quite apart from that which we call the tender passion. If Berlioz had first seen Harriet in Southerne's *Isabella, or the Fatal Marriage*—the play in which she failed four days before his concert of 9 December 1832—I much question whether she would have made the same impression on him. Seeing that the actress had seemingly been unsullied by the breath of slander during the time she played in Kemble's company, true love would not have believed the *affreuses vérités* so readily. Berlioz was not the only man who admired the beautiful actress. Her dressing-room must have been a bower of flowers; had she retained all her presents she might have stocked a jeweller's shop; sumptuous apartments were placed at her disposal. Yet her life was exemplary. But Berlioz's love was an essentially artificial one, in keeping with that found in the novels of the time, many of which glorified a hopeless attachment. His infatuation wilted when he met Camille and was plunged into a genuine love. And whatever her mother may have schemed, whatever she may have become eventually, I cannot believe that Camille was only playing a part. For some short time at least she loved Berlioz as far as her shallow nature admitted.

The concert of 9 December must have been one of the most dramatic in the annals of music. Every one must have been in a state of tension. The audience, knowing the story of Berlioz and Harriet and the programme of the work intended to vilify the latter, must have been wondering if they were to witness some scene, ludicrous or scandalous. Harriet, in her box, pleased to be the cynosure of every eye, and hoping that this unexpected publicity might in some way change her theatrical failure into a success, that if the Parisians would not come to see her as Isabella, they would be curious to see her as the heroine of a symphony. As she was not musical, the passionate phrases of the first movement and the devilish variation of the

ideé fixe (*her* motive) in the last would alike fail to
move her. Any attempt to describe the turmoil of
Berlioz's emotions would be futile. Everything con-
spired to arouse in him a determination to marry this
woman who had indirectly contributed to his musical
triumph. And the opposition he encountered only
strengthened his determination. Romain Rolland is
inclined to dwell on Berlioz's weakness as regards
women, and possibly he may have exhibited a certain
amount with respect to Marie Recio, though he was
by no means the first man to find it impossible to
discard a mistress. With Harriet, however, he displayed some of the qualities associated with the
proverbial cave-man. His previous attempt at marriage
had failed through no fault of his own. He would not
be baulked a second time. His family were horrified
at the idea of his marrying an actress, and his father
absolutely refused his consent. To enable him to
marry, French law demanded that he should resort to
the unpleasant operation of serving on Dr. Berlioz
three *sommations respectueuses*, a rare occurrence in respectable families. The first of these was in February
1833, two months after he had been introduced to
Harriet, and before the lady had definitely given her
consent. The impetuosity of our prophet knew no
bounds! And it contrasts astoundingly with the
patient care he devoted to his musical compositions.
His friends sympathized with him, but they could not
have approved of this marriage with a woman, who
had broken her leg—on 1 March—and was heavily
in debt, owing to the failure of her theatrical venture;
and Harriet's hump-backed sister bitterly opposed the
match. The course of love, true or false, certainly did
not run smooth. As Berlioz told Ferrand in a letter
of 30 August 'scenes became more violent', and once,
when Harriet reproached him with not loving her,
he endeavoured to commit suicide, a statement upon
which M. Boschot casts doubts, obsessed by the idea

that Berlioz was incapable of telling the truth even to his best friend. Neither Hippeau nor Jullien, however, appears to question it, and the action is in keeping with the composer's behaviour at that time. It was not a great step from imagining the programme of his symphony to actually carrying it out. The letter to Ferrand goes on to say that Harriet still wavered, and that he had sent her an ultimatum. If she still refused he would depart for Berlin, his passport being already obtained.

'To help me to endure this horrible separation [he was evidently anticipating Harriet's refusal] an incredible piece of luck has thrown into my arms a poor young girl of eighteen, who fled four years ago from a wretch who had bought her as a child, and, until four years back, had kept her in a state of bondage; she is frightened to death at the idea of falling again into the hands of this monster, and declares that she would rather throw herself into the river than return to her proprietor.'

He then describes the girl's attractions, and says that he intends to ask Spontini to take her into the chorus of the Berlin Opera House. 'If she loves me, I will wring my heart to express some semblance of love.' M. Boschot suggests that the so-called slave was a fraud, and that the fairy-tale was invented by Jules Janin and other of Berlioz's friends in the hopes of extricating the musician from an undesirable marriage. It may well be so! I have quoted Berlioz's letter principally to emphasize his extraordinary guilelessness. Few men of thirty would have swallowed such a story. Saint-Saëns was correct in insisting on the naïvety of Berlioz. In his music he was a genius, a man of commanding stature: in the everyday affairs of life he, like many other geniuses, was too often little more than a headstrong child, yet lovable withal, and with a child's inability to count the cost.

Hippeau and others, swayed by Legouvé's recollections, assert that Berlioz, by his constant infidelities, gave his wife ample justification for her terrible jealousy. Against Legouvé's indictment we may set the doubts of M. Étienne Rey : 'Are we to believe, as we are assured by one of his best friends, that during this troublous time Berlioz abandoned himself to a number of fugitive amours, to those short temporary connexions which are part of theatrical life ? No other witness save this one, no allusion, no letters, not a word of Berlioz, so expansive and so indiscreet, supports him or confirms him."[1] As M. Rey's book belongs to a series devoted to the amorous lives of eminent people, the author can be trusted to have used his best efforts to unveil any scandal for which there was a shadow of warranty. As I have pointed out, Legouvé, the only witness, was not entirely trustworthy; and, in this case, he probably heard only Harriet's version. Men are considered by the opposite sex to 'hang together'. But when a woman with a dramatic training pours into a man's ear the tale of her husband's turpitude, I fear, alas! that he is only too ready to believe even his best friend a sad rascal. And Harriet was a beautiful woman, and belonged to the same theatrical world as Legouvé. Berlioz's business as a critic brought him daily into contact with many singers and actresses, and she, knowing theatrical life as it was in Paris in those days, would be tempted to be jealous, even if she were not by nature prone to that meanest of all sins. Had she been able to enjoy some triumphs of her own, matters might have been different. She plagued her husband to obtain engagements for her, but all her appearances on 'the boards' were failures. Even her Mad Scene, which had created such a sensation in 1827, was received with cat-calls, when she played it at some benefit performance. Moralists may condemn Berlioz for leaving his wife, but his subsequent behaviour was commendable. He provided for her, saw that she had every attention during her illnesses, which were aggra-

---

[1] *La Vie amoureuse de Berlioz*, Paris, 1929.

vated, if not caused, by her intemperate habits, and continued to pay her friendly calls from time to time. Three days after her death on 3 March 1854, he wrote to his sister Adèle (the dots being his own, and not indicative of omissions):

'How horrible is life! . . . Memories, bitter and sweet, pass through my mind at the same time! Her grand qualities, her cruel unreasonableness, her injustices, but then her genius and her misfortunes! . . . Horrible! Terrible! I cannot weep. She taught me to understand Shakespeare and great dramatic art. She shared misery with me, she never hesitated when it was necessary to risk our necessaries for some musical enterprise . . . then, opposed to this courage, she was always against my leaving Paris, she would not allow me to travel; if I had not taken drastic measures I should to-day be still unknown in Europe. . . . And her jealousy *without reason* which finally was the cause of all that changed my life.' [1]

As Adèle was naturally fully cognizant of her brother's relations with Marie Recio, he obviously was excluding them from his real or imaginary infidelities. Harriet had made his life unbearable, and when at last he left her he considered himself free to choose another companion. Legouvé, though biased in her favour, does not give a particularly attractive picture of Harriet's behaviour. Having explained that her initial coldness had become an ardent flame; while Berlioz's passion for her had died down to a 'sincere friendship, calm and correct', he proceeds:

'Madame Berlioz searched his feuilletons for traces of his infidelities; she searched for them also elsewhere, and fragments of intercepted letters, drawers indiscreetly left unlocked provided her with inconclusive proofs which were sufficient to make her beside herself, but only told her half the truth. The heart of Berlioz travelled so quickly that she was unable to follow it. When, owing to her researches, she discovered the object of his passion, that passion had changed, and then his actual innocence was easy to prove.'

[1] *Au milieu du chemin* (ed. Julien Tiersot), Paris, 1930.

While feeling confident that the above describes the conduct of Harriet, I, in accord with M. Étienne Rey, distrust it profoundly as presenting a faithful picture of the composer. Berlioz's life was not immaculate, but I cannot think that he was such a *coureur de dames* as Legouvé pretends. On the other hand, many cf us have known that wife of a musical or dramatic critic who scents infidelity whenever her husband praises the performance of some actress or singer. The suggestion that Berlioz was able to prove his innocence as regards Mademoiselle X., because he had forsaken her for Mademoiselle Y., is highly ingenious, but not absolutely convincing. Hippeau apostrophizes Harriet thus: 'Poor innocent flower gathered in her grace and freshness, who remained henceforth without support, without a look, languishing and wilting on its stem, and drooped, withered and died, because the hand that should have tended her abandoned her to pluck others!' This 'sob-stuff' has no other warranty than the word of one man, a dramatist who would be apt to think in terms of the stage and imagine situations that had no foundation in fact. The prosecutors of Berlioz do not always inquire into the credibility of their witnesses. And, since the world has lost a symphony from the pen of Berlioz, because the sum required for its production had to be employed on nurses and medical attendance for Harriet, when she might have been sent to a hospital, to declare that she was left 'without support' is untrue. Personally, I cannot imagine an 'innocent flower' ransacking her husband's belongings, burning to discover some justification for her insensate jealousy.

As regards Marie Recio it was another matter. When Berlioz met her first we do not know. She appeared at the Opéra in the small role of Inès in *La Favorite* on 5 November 1841, probably owing to his influence. We know very little of his private life from December 1840 to December 1842—the mysterious years, as M. Boschot calls them—and

therefore are free to exercise our imagination, coloured
by our measure of sympathy for the composer. In
his Memoirs he says he went to Brussels in 1840,
whereas he did not go there till September 1842: he
heads his first tour in Germany '1841–1842', when
in reality it was 1842–3. Hippeau imputes these
inexactitudes to some deep design on the part of the
writer to befog his readers concerning his rupture with
Harriet—it is difficult to see how! Jullien, more
reasonably, attributes them to a faulty memory. In
one of his letters to his son, Berlioz admits that he
has no head for figures; and one only has to read his
letters to realize his vagueness in respect to dates.
He is often doubtful as to the date of the month, and
even at times as to that of the century. M. Boschot
admits that he relied on Legouvé for his account of
Berlioz's matrimonial troubles—there is no other witness—and describes him (in a footnote) as 'that faithful
friend, who received the confidences of Berlioz, and
assisted him oftener than one would credit'. In this
case, however, the playwright gives no hint that he
had received any confidences from Berlioz! M. Boschot
then gives rein to his imagination, as he does in other
places when he is without his 'tons of paper', an
imagination similar to that which he professes to deplore
in Berlioz. He talks of 'the various women of the
stage, singers, dancers, supers, who had caused such
suffering to poor Ophelia'. Very sad! But how unfortunate that no Leporello can be produced to specify
the achievements of this Don Juan of the Parisian
world of the 1830's! M. Boschot then proceeds to
sketch Berlioz's life during those mysterious years,
very plausibly, but entirely without documentary corroboration. Marie Martin—Recio was only a stage
name—and her mother were excellent housewives, and
we can quite imagine the harassed husband finding in
their orderly household the peace denied him at home.
Both M. Boschot and Hippeau take it for granted that

Marie was Berlioz's mistress long before she accompanied him to Brussels in September 1842. But she was an astute young person, who would be unlikely to join in the general scramble for Berlioz's handkerchief, such as is suggested by his faithful friend, Legouvé. If we indulge in flights of fancy, it is not difficult to picture Marie eluding her lover until she was assured that he was separated from his wife. It is true that Berlioz, in announcing his marriage to Marie in 1854 to his brother-in-law Suat, said that he had lived with her for fourteen years, i.e. since 1840. But, though this is in agreement with the erroneous dates of the Memoirs, which he was on the point of completing,[1] we know that it was not literally true. (This clinging to inaccurate dates, even in a private letter, supports Jullien's contention that they were simply owing to a faulty memory.) He returned to Harriet after his Brussels concerts, but did not remain for long. In the December he again left her, departing stealthily for Germany, and apparently intending to go alone. He had no desire for Marie's companionship. She would hamper him in many ways; and the musician dreaded her singing of his music. She was, however, too clever for him, and, to give her her due, as his cashier and bookkeeper, she probably saved him more than her board and lodging. There is no need to insist again on Berlioz's care for Harriet after their separation, nor on his grief at her death. He, like many another artist, was probably a somewhat difficult man to live with (although Marie managed to do so with a fair amount of success); but the root of all their trouble was the jealousy of a rather stupid woman—judging by her letters, she never succeeded in learning French, though no doubt she was fluent enough, especially as regards invective.

[1] The date at the end of the Memoirs, as originally intended, is 18 Oct. 1854. The Post-Scriptum, Postface, and *Voyage en Dauphiné* were added later.

To turn to Berlioz's healthy normal love for Camille is to leave the stifling heat of a hot-house for the fragrance of a garden. He was not entirely a free agent as regards Harriet: his love for her was confused with too many other things. *Der Mensch kann was er will; er kann nicht aber wollen was er will.* The composer could will to marry Harriet or not; but he could not will his will, which was dependent on his temperament, his emotions, his ideas, in a way which only a psychiatrist could unravel. On the other hand, his love for Camille ran the course of the majority of love-affairs— the couple met, became enamoured one of the other, became engaged, and the wedding was fixed at a not very distant date. If, as Hiller suggests, Madame Moke had already arranged to marry her daughter to Pleyel before Berlioz left for Italy, she concealed her intentions very cleverly, even admitting that the musician was easy to deceive. When he was held a prisoner in the Institute, during the composition of the cantata that gained him the *prix de Rome*, she sent her maid Désirée to inquire after him, and I cannot think that this was the only evidence of her apparent liking for him. In any case Berlioz left for Rome at the end of 1830, firmly persuaded that in two years' time Camille would become his wife, that she would be that sympathetic companion whom he sought in vain all his life. He remains in Rome till the April, gnawing out his heart, and expecting by every post the letter that never arrives. Unable to bear the suspense any longer, he sets out for France, fully aware that in doing so he will probably lose his pension. He reaches Florence, and there has an an attack of quinsy, which one must have experienced to realize how one's vitality is lowered, to say nothing of the wearying pain. In this condition he receives an abominable letter from Madame Moke, and determines on murder. How he would have acted, had he been in a state of robust health, we can only guess, though it is not without significance that, when he anticipated Harriet's refusal to marry him, he was prepared to accept it in a philosophical manner. In dealing with his mad escapade, sufficient stress has not been laid on those three months of constant worry followed by the quinsy.

The whole story of Berlioz's adventure will never be known, since we lack his letters to Ferrand written at the time. Their recipient, horrified at the tale of contemplated bloodshed, probably destroyed them at once. I am inclined to think that what turned Berlioz from his purpose can be gathered from his letter to Horace Vernet, the Principal of the French Academy at Rome, when he begged that his pension might not be withdrawn, and swore on his honour not to leave Italy. Bernard[1] quotes from a fragment of this letter, then in the possession of the Baron de Triment, which must obviously be a rough draft, since M. Boschot[2] gives the letter complete from the collection of Charles Malherbe. The wording of the fragment differs from the actual letter in two respects only, *odieux* for *hidieux*, and *vu* instead of *cru*, which may be a clerical error, but somewhat alters the sense—'they saw me fall' instead 'they thought I fell'. Here is an extract from the letter, as given by M. Boschot.

'I write to you in haste . . . a hideous crime, *an abuse of confidence* of which I have been the victim has made me beside myself since I left Florence. I flew to France to carry out the most just and most terrible revenge; at Genoa, a moment of giddiness, the most incredible weakness, destroyed my will-power, I gave way to the despair of a child; but I escaped with a drink of salt water, being gaffed like a salmon, lying dead in the sun for a quarter of an hour, and with violent sickness for an hour; I do not know who rescued me; they thought I fell by accident from the ramparts of the town.'

M. Boschot, inspired by Charles Malherbe (to whom he acknowledges his indebtedness for every page of

1 *Notice sur Berlioz* heading the *Correspondance inédite.*
2 *La Jeunesse d'un romantique.*

his book), takes this attempted suicide of Berlioz's during 'a moment of giddiness' (a very probable result of a quinsy combined with lack of food) as a fiction. First, on the general principle that, except when it suits one's purpose to believe them, one must mistrust all Berlioz's statements ; secondly, that he was loth to return to Rome empty-handed, as it were. If he could not figure as a triple murderer, wanted by the police, he might 'save his face' by a frustrated suicide. I cannot see why he need have troubled to lie to Vernet, who must have acted as father-confessor to many. Berlioz had left Rome not knowing what he was about to do. I have already given a good reason why he was reticent as regards his adventure. Something induced Berlioz to relinquish his scheme of revenge ; and I am willing to believe his tale, because an hour's vomiting seems an excellent method of diverting a musician's thoughts. That he seriously intended to kill both Camille and her 'hippopotamus' of a mother, there can be no doubt : I take it to be equally certain that their conduct embittered his life. A man may accept a woman's refusal with tolerable equanimity, and, if he meets her in later life, may feel inclined to thank her for it. But many men become misanthropes owing to being jilted, and their feelings are intensified if the jilting takes place almost on the steps of the altar. We have the testimony of Mendelssohn as to how much Berlioz counted on his marriage. He had conceived a hopeless passion for Estelle, which, thirty years later, he still shuddered to think of ; his attempt to win Harriet had proved fruitless ; and now to be thrown over by a girl on whom he had bestowed a perfectly honest affection, one whom he had met in everyday life, away from the glare of the footlights and unconnected with anything outside herself ! With his weakness for petty vengeances, it was unlikely that Camille should escape his pen. He portrayed her twice ; once in *Le Suicide par enthusiasme*, in which he

figures as Adolphe D——, a young musician devoted
to Gluck and an enthusiastic admirer of *La Vestale*,
while Camille is Hortense N——, a kind of immoral
Mrs. Leo Hunter, always ready to fling herself at the
head of the latest celebrity. In *Euphonia*, which ran
through the pages of *La Gazette musicale* of 1844, he
treats his sometime fiancée more brutally, so much
so that it is difficult to find excuses for him unless we
charitably suppose that his resentment was still so
burning as to make him forget himself. In the novel
Camille appears under her own name backwards
(Ellimac), while he himself is Rotceh (Hector reversed), Madame Moke, with execrable taste, figuring
as Madame Ellianac (*Canaille* backwards). When the
tale afterwards appeared in *Les Soirées de l'orchestre*
Berlioz had the grace to choose other names. The
novel, which incidentally includes an interesting account of an imaginary town devoted entirely to music,
concludes with the crushing to death in an ingeniously
constructed steel pavilion of Ellimac, her mother,
some of her lovers, and a number of women whose
reputation matched her own.

At a concert in London on 28 April 1852 Camille
(Madame Pleyel) and Berlioz met for probably the
first time since she was his Ariel—he as conductor,
she as the soloist of Weber's *Concertstück*. Apparently
the orchestral playing was rough, and, on one occasion,
the lady complained, the orchestra crashed in a bar
or two too soon, which she attributed to spite on the
part of her rejected lover. Francis Hueffer, in relating
the tale,[1] refuses to 'attribute such meanness to the
great composer'. In so far as his action was probably
not deliberate, I agree. Berlioz had too much admiration for Weber to play tricks with his works. It seems
to me more probable that the hypersensitive musician,
thrown into unwilling contact with the woman who
had caused him so much unhappiness, had to exercise

[1] *Half a Century of Music in England*, London, 1889.

all his will-power to control himself, and was physically incapable of properly controlling the orchestra.

If Berlioz's love-affair with Camille Moke had not been terminated by the tragi-comic *Épisode bouffon*, commentators might be disposed to appreciate more fully the disastrous effect she had on his life. His habit of treasuring up a wrong—and, as in the case of Charles Blanc, a kindness—aggravated by his temperamental aloofness, his *mal de l'isolement*, is clear proof of his inability to forget. And persistent dwelling on a wrong must affect one's outlook on life. As Berlioz, when penning his Memoirs, was not writing his Confessions, we cannot expect to find in them (or even in his letters) much evidence to support my contention. There can be no question, however, as to Estelle influencing his life, and it is reasonable to suppose that the influence of the woman who dealt him such a shattering blow would be equally strong.

To leave the man and to deal with the legends connected with the musician, we are confronted by a number of obsessions that are difficult, if not impossible, to disturb, because, like all obsessions, they are irremovable by reason. That the Parisians of the 1830's, who found Beethoven incomprehensible, should consider Berlioz's music 'eccentric' and 'extravagant' is understandable. But much water has flowed under the Pont Neuf and other bridges during the past hundred years. And nowadays to insist on the 'extravagances of Berlioz, beside which Hugo is reticent', as has been done in a recent standard work, makes one 'rather tired', to quote Mr. Ernest Newman, who close on thirty years ago in his admirable article on Berlioz in *Musical Studies* reeled off an almost complete list of the composer's output, concluding: 'Out of all these thousands of pages, how ridiculously few of them deserve the epithet of "extravagance"; of how many of them is it true that

Berlioz's "eloquence pours forth in a turbid, impetuous torrent which levels all obstacles and overpowers all restraint"?' The sentence quoted by Mr. Newman is prefaced by the statement that Berlioz's 'imagination seems always at white heat'; it appears both in an earlier edition and the present one of the standard work. Time evidently has not modified the writer's opinion. It would be of interest to know precisely what he means. If an imagination at white heat means that Berlioz was always divinely inspired, even the French master's warmest admirers would be prepared to contradict flatly such an assumption. If it means that Berlioz usually dashed off his compositions, and therefore they are in the nature of extempores, the patient care he devoted to them and the retouches he made prove the contrary. It is to be feared that the 'imagination at white heat' and the torrent of his eloquence 'which levels all obstacles'—an expression which, by the way, might be applied at times to Beethoven—have their origin in a confusion between the artist and the man. Given a musician who made a practice of suicide and spent his spare time in planning murders, perhaps it is not unnatural to read into his music the same 'volcanic' qualities. Yet 'volcanic' is as misleading an epithet to apply to him as 'romantic'. The obsession that he was essentially a *romantic* composer —whatever that implies exactly—has led to distorted performances of his works. Their virility has been transmogrified into a sickly sentimentality. It was refreshing lately, after a stage performance of *The Damnation of Faust*, to find that excellent critic, Mr. Richard Capell, drawing attention to the greatness of the music 'so inventive, so varied, and so cleanly classical!' Cleanly classical! The term can be applied to even his pictures of demons and brigands. The former are not those of pantomime, while the latter belie the horrible description of the finale of the *Harold in Italy* Symphony which Berlioz, with his tongue in his

cheek, gave to Heine in the open letter to the poet
in the Memoirs.

This reference to the horrible brings us to another
legend regarding Berlioz, one closely linked with his
'extravagance', that, apart from anything else, his
fondness for depicting the gruesome is sufficient to
exclude him from the ranks of the greatest masters.
I once troubled[1] to combat this curious idea by means
of statistics. In the unfinished German edition there
are 2,904 pages of orchestral score, setting aside the
arrangements. Had the edition been completed by the
addition of *The Trojans, Benvenuto Cellini,* and other
works, the probable total number of pages would be
4,000. On an extravagantly liberal estimate, framed
to suit the most timid member of an audience, the
'creepy' pages cannot exceed 200—five per cent of
the whole. As a matter of fact, I doubt whether a
healthy-minded auditor could find in Berlioz even a
hundred pages that can justifiably be described as horrible, in the sense that some of Poe's tales (forming a
small percentage of his collected works) are, or many
of Wiertz's pictures. I was too anxious to oblige the
timid listener, since I included in my list of horrors
such numbers as the whole of the 'Judex crederis' of the
Te Deum (omitting only the 'Salvum fac'), and the whole
of the March to Execution and the Witches' Sabbath.
M. Paul Morillot[2] speaks of *la douloureuse Marche au Supplice,* and though 'dolorous' is not the epithet I should
myself apply to the movement, it fits it better than
'horrible' or 'gruesome'. Commentators have sought
to justify their description by imagining (quite gratui-
tously) a gory-minded crowd of *sans-culottes* and *trico-
teuses.* There is no warranty, however, for supposing
that the hero of the symphony in his opium-dream
was transported back to the Reign of Terror. The
action of the work took place at the then present day

---

[1] 'Berlioz the Blood-curdler', *The Musical Mirror,* Nov. 1930.
[2] *Berlioz écrivain,* Grenoble, 1903.

(1830). Whether criminals were actually marched through the streets of Paris to the Place de la Grève at that date, I do not know. Something must be allowed for poetic licence ! Berlioz, feeling music so deeply, at times undoubtedly employed extravagant terms to describe his own. But we must not take them too literally! Considering the composer's skill in depicting what may be called the horrible in its largest sense, it is a matter for surprise that he did not indulge it more freely.

The legend of Berlioz's 'somewhat haphazard musical education' will be dealt with in the next chapter. It need be only remarked here that, if a young man spent four years at the R.A.M. (or R.C.M.) and left in a state of abysmal ignorance, it would reflect on the teachers rather than the pupil, unless the latter chanced to be a hopeless idiot or incorrigibly lazy. Now, Berlioz was certainly not an idiot, and we have not a shred of evidence that he was lazy.

This present chapter may well end with an account of a legend in the making. In *La Revue de Paris* for 1906 Paul Viardot (son of the celebrated singer) brought out his *Souvenirs d'un artiste*, which appeared later in book form. On p. 4 of the latter we read :

'Berlioz came there [the Château de Courtavenel, the home of the Viardots] to work with my mother, who rendered him the inestimable service of correcting his basses. For, astonishing as it may appear, that great man totally lacked the instinct for the true ones. *The Taking of Troy* and *The Trojans* [*sic*] were accordingly completely revised by my mother.'

The story is repeated by Jean Huré,[1] from whom M. Masson quotes, in a footnote to his *Berlioz*. Now, right or wrong, Berlioz's basses were part of his musical thought, and, as he always resented any aspersion on his system of harmony, it is extremely improbable that at the end of his career he would have borne with patience criticism of his basses from any

[1] 'Berlioz musicien', *La Renaissance contemporaine*, 10 Dec. 1911.

one. As Paul Viardot was a schoolboy of thirteen
during the war of 1870–1 his testimony to what
Berlioz may or may not have done in 1858 (the date
of the completion of *The Trojans* and the writing of
the piano arrangement) is valueless. Many writers on
Berlioz are, however, quite prepared to put puling
infants into the witness-box, if they fancy that thereby
they can injure the French master's reputation. Since
it is difficult to picture Berlioz inviting an audience
to assist at the pretended harmonyl essons, Madame
Viardot was the only person who could support her
son's tale; and she, in 1906, was an old lady of
eighty-five, an age at which one is rather apt to invent stories to one's credit. It is true that she might
have told the tale for twenty years. But there chances
to be a respectable witness on the other side.
These supposed lessons had at any rate an audience
of one.

An interview with Saint-Saëns appeared in the
Journal de musique of 25 November 1876,[1] over which
Paul Viardot should have pondered before he made
too positive a statement. Having pointed out that the
arrangement of the Royal Hunt is better than that of
the rest, and how Berlioz, mistrusting arrangers and
anxious to avoid technical difficulties, created new ones
from his ignorance of the piano, Saint-Saëns went on
to relate how the composer struggled with his self-
imposed task up to the scene in question. Here he
had to acknowledge defeat. 'A celebrated pianist [one
wonders who it was], to whom he applied, was no
more competent. He then confided his trouble to
Mme Viardot, who begged to be allowed to undertake
the work, and she succeeded where the composer and
the celebrated pianist had failed.' 'With my very own
eyes', Saint-Saëns assured the interviewer, 'I have
seen Mme Viardot, pen in hand, eyes aflame, the

[1] I am indebted to M. Tiersot's 'Berlioziana' (*Le Ménestrel*, 9 July
1905) for my knowledge of the interview.

manuscript of *The Trojans* on her piano, writing the arrangement of the Royal Hunt.'

Somehow or other, Saint-Saëns's account, related only eight years after the event, instead of thirty-eight, rings truer.

There is a similar tale about a certain professor of the Conservatoire named Barthe, who, we are told, 'assisted' Berlioz in his harmony after about 1850. As the rumour must have originated with Barthe himself, it is satisfactory to know that even at that date there was a professor who admired Berlioz's harmony so much that he wished to claim a hand in it.

Chapter Three

TECHNIQUE

THE dreams of an artist in poem, music, or picture can never be fully realized. Whatever be the medium, it is never delicate enough to express his ideas as he conceived them. At the commencement of his career the inadequacy of his weapons may not be apparent even to himself. He employs those of his predecessors, and these, with a few characteristic alterations (which we often can perceive only after we have studied his later works), suffice him. It is when he has reached the summit of his creative powers that he chafes at his inability to convey to others the precise texture of his dreams; and by this time he has become so accustomed to the weapons he has hitherto used that he can seldom avail himself of new ones. It is true that in his progress he has effected many changes in his armoury—discarding this, remodelling that, adding much forged by himself—but it still remains essentially the same, and he is forced to cling to it. Modern harmony, modern orchestration, and the skill of modern performers on modern instruments constitute a more perfect vehicle of expression than that which Beethoven possessed. Yet, had he been in command of such resources previous to the composition of (say) the Eroica Symphony, it is doubtful whether the work would be greater than it is. Indeed the reverse is probable.

Berlioz was in a different category from any other composer in that, at the beginning of his career, he found the weapons of such of his predecessors as he knew of little service to him. For the expression of his ideas he had to devise weapons of his own, and this while he was still a student and unskilled in the manipulation of those in current usage. That he so soon found himself is a testimony to his genius. His

detractors are charitably inclined to impute his deviations from the text-books of his time to two causes.
First, to the fact that he did not begin his serious studies
until late in life ; and secondly, that during the four
years he spent at the Conservatoire he was idle. We
may dismiss the first reason. Berlioz may have been
eighteen before he received any instruction in harmony
—from Gerono, a private pupil of Lesueur. But Schumann was older still ; and Wagner, although he was
two years younger, was on his own showing not a
satisfactory pupil. As for some of the Russian composers, they seem to have dispensed with serious
training altogether. I doubt much whether those same
detractors, if they were apprehensive about the condition of their livers, would refrain from consulting a
Harley Street physician on the grounds that he had
not commenced his study of anatomy and *materia
medica* at the tender age of seven. Yet these are subjects of infinitely greater complexity than harmony
and counterpoint.

As to the second suggestion, there is no authority
for believing Berlioz to have been a lazy student. It
is true that we know practically nothing of his days
at the Conservatoire. He was probably inclined to be
argumentative, but there is no reason for supposing
that he neglected his exercises, if only out of regard
for his two masters. He had an affection for Lesueur,
who taught him harmony, and at any rate entertained
a respect for Reicha, who instructed him in fugue and
counterpoint.

Unfortunately, Lesueur's system of harmony,
founded on that of Rameau, did not appeal to Berlioz.
In his Memoirs he tells us that as a boy he attempted
the study of Rameau's treatise, and failed to understand it. His first insight into harmony was obtained
from Catel's treatise, the standard one of the day, and
from hearing the quartets of Haydn and the elder Pleyel.
To chapter vi of the Memoirs he adds a footnote in

which he refers contemptuously to Rameau's theories, based on the vibrations of a *corde sonore*, 'which he [Rameau] calls the sonorous body, as though strings were the only vibrating bodies in the universe ; or rather, as if the theory of their vibrations were applicable to the resonance of all other sonorous bodies'. In all probability Berlioz in the matter of harmony derived greater benefit from the teachings of Reicha, who could have scarcely avoided touching on the subject, though strictly speaking it was outside his province. Lesueur was undoubtedly an excellent master—as witness his thirteen other pupils who gained the *prix de Rome*—but he was too much influenced by what he believed to have been the harmony of the Greeks, Hebrews, and Egyptians.[1] Reicha, on the other hand, though not possessing a tithe of the genius of the composer of *Les Bardes*, was one of the first to realize than any theory of harmony should be derived from the practice of the masters.

In spite, however, of Berlioz's inability to swallow the Rameau-cum-Lesueur system of harmony, he could not have had a better mentor than the old composer, himself a revolutionist in his time, and better able to understand his 'volcanic' pupil than any other musician in Paris. None other than he could have been so far-seeing as to glimpse something of Berlioz's future greatness from his first crude attempts. How far Lesueur influenced his successor, it were hard to say, since it was principally as regards ideas. That is, while it is possible to trace certain features of Berlioz's work to the teachings of his master, we cannot say of any number that it suggests Lesueur in the same way as it may faintly recall Gluck or Beethoven.

Too much stress has been laid on the faults—real or imaginary—in Berlioz's harmony, and too little on its

[1] Lesueur's *La Mort d'Adam* is perhaps the most curious score in existence, page after page being filled with long disquisitions in French or Italian on the meaning and use of the different chords.

excellences. To harp on imperfections obviously due to inexperience seems an unnecessary waste of time that would be more profitably employed in comparing the Fantastic Symphony, composed in Berlioz's student days, with similar works of the other masters —examples for the moment evade me!—that are performed as frequently, and exhibit as much original genius, even purely from the technical point of view. Indeed, Jean Marnold, one of the most virulent of Berlioz's antagonists, admits that 'he wrote better at twenty-seven (1830—the Fantastic Symphony) than Wagner at twenty-eight (1841—*The Flying Dutchman*)'.[1] Schumann's remarks on the harmony of the Fantastic Symphony are of value as coming from a contemporary less hide-bound than Fétis and some other Parisian critics. But we must not forget that Schumann's criticism of the French master's work was written to enable him to obtain his doctor's degree, and that his examiners would probably possess academic, if not pedantic, ideas. He must have wondered whether his approval of so much of the harmony would be echoed by his judges. He was hampered in his criticism, and the more so because, as he is careful to point out, he had only the piano score before him. The remarks of the eminent theorist, M. Charles Kœchlin, have considerably more weight. He not only knows the whole of Berlioz's output, and therefore realizes at what the young composer was aiming in his early symphony, but also has an exhaustive acquaintance with modern harmony and thus can appreciate any suggestions of it found in Berlioz's scores. In his *Traité de l'harmonie* M. Kœchlin[2] says:

'Berlioz, while claiming complete liberty, was not an anarchist, nor even a revolutionist. He appeared to be such to con-

[1] 'Hector Berlioz "Musicien"', *Mercure de France*, 15 Jan. and 1 Feb. 1905.
[2] M. Charles Kœchlin, although practically unknown in England, must be counted amongst the greatest of living theorists. As Mr. Calvocoressi

temporaries ignorant of the harmony of Beethoven, Mozart, and Bach; but Berlioz's chords are of the same family as those of his illustrious German compeers. The sentiment indeed may be occasionally different, and one finds a foreshadowing of modern times. It is in this most frequently that his novelty consists.'

That is, Berlioz was a pioneer in harmony as he was in other ways. In at least one respect many modern composers might learn much from him, and that is as regards the expressive value of common chords.

Some of Berlioz's deviations from the academic rules of his day must be ascribed to his unconscious originality. It is folly to pretend that he did not know the rules! He *felt* such-and-such a progression, and, as Schumann says, while a tyro could 'correct' it, the alteration would often entail a loss of effect. Some of his methods, such as a certain rigidity of bass-line, may be traced to his early admiration of Gluck and Spontini. But I am inclined to think that possibly his harmony owed something to his practice of the guitar, the only instrument he ever really learnt, his powers of execution on the flute (his earliest instrument) being probably limited. One reads at times of infant prodigies, who are able to name at once any note or any combination of notes that may be played to them. The ordinary person, however, even though he may have music in his soul, has to be taught to distinguish between one chord and another, and to recognize the difference between the several inversions of the same chord. And this he learns from listening to a piano. Gradually he learns to rely on his mental ear for the

said of him (*Musical Times*, Oct. 1930), he is 'a composer and teacher of sound judgement and wide experience, endowed with an altogether unusual gift for harmonic invention'. He is the composer of over a hundred works (list in *The Dominant*, Feb. 1929), including a large number of chorales, a treatise on Counterpoint, and another on Harmony (3 vols.), the latter undoubtedly one of the best and most exhaustive ever written.

sound of the various combinations. But, as Mr. R. O.
Morris has so clearly expressed it :[1]

'The most unpromising collocation of notes may turn into a
chord, whose precise effect in a particular context probably cannot be forejudged; it may have to be tried experimentally at
the piano, whose role in the extension and development of harmonic resource has been of incalculable importance. Formerly
a composer who used the piano in this way was supposed for
some obscure reason not to be quite playing the game. This
form of snobbery is now a thing of the past; a modern composer's obligation to his piano is no matter for pride or shame,
but is simply taken for granted.'

The need to test chords at the piano varies greatly with
different musicians, and bears no relation to their
musical talent. The objection to this reliance on the
keyboard, continually at the commencement of a
musician's career and occasionally in later life, is that
he cannot avoid a tendency to think in terms of the
piano. Parenthetically it might be added that in the
second case the testing is not always confined to a
single chord; a pianist is tempted to 'try over' the
whole or part of the movement. Saint-Saëns tells us
that at one time he was accustomed to call on Gounod
every morning in order to play over what the elder
composer had written the night before, since the latter
was not clever at playing from score. Even in the
works of the greatest orchestrators we find reminiscences of keyboard practice in passages given to the
harps, violins, and other instruments. And, while undoubtedly harmony would not be where it is without
the assistance of the piano or organ, at times they may
prove to be snares. Chords and progressions which
on them are highly effective may lose much of their
value when transferred to the orchestra; and, con-
versely, chords and progressions that are excellent on
the orchestra may sound thin and poor on the piano.
Practically all musicians being tarred with the same

[1] 'An Introduction to Music' in *An Outline of Modern Knowledge*.

brush, pianistic platitudes which would be glaringly apparent to a Berlioz who had not learnt a keyboard instrument, to them are negligible and often unnoticed. If, however, they are more at home on the piano than the organ, they will frequently detect suggestions of organ practice in orchestral scores. How much more then are they apt to be uneasily aware of habits founded on guitar practice, even though they may be ignorant of the reason for their uneasiness?

To avoid misapprehension, I hasten to explain that, beyond a fondness for pizzicato,[1] there is no trace of the guitar in Berlioz's orchestration. Every instrument is given a part admirably fitted to its particular requirements. We cannot point to passages that are essentially guitar passages as we can at times in the scores of many other composers pick out pages that undoubtedly have been conceived in terms of the keyboard. Even Berlioz's harmony is purely orchestral. It is in his choice of chords and possibly their occasional resolution that I would find a subtle connexion with the fact of part of his ear-training being derived from the guitar.

There are several kinds of guitar, the best known being the Spanish guitar, which possesses six strings, the lowest (the 6th) being tuned to E below the bass clef, and those above it to A, D, G, B, and E.[2] Its music is written in the treble clef, an octave above the real sounds. The three lowest strings are 'covered' (like the G string of a violin) and are played by the thumb alone: the three highest are of plain gut, and are plucked by the first, second, and third fingers. The compass is three and a half octaves. From this

---

[1] Berlioz was anxious to establish a class for pizzicato at the Conservatoire, in order that violinists might be taught to use fingers other than the first one, as is usual in orchestras.

[2] The tuning is subject to variation. Thus, for a piece in E major (a favourite key for the instrument) the 3rd string (G) may be sharpened, and the 4th and 5th (D and A) raised a tone, as is intended for the serenade of Mephistopheles in *Eight Scenes from Faust*.

rough description it will be seen that chords must be arranged in a manner differing considerably from that on a keyboard instrument. When the youthful Berlioz endeavoured to teach himself the sound of the various chords, the resolution of the discords, and so on, as set forth in Catel's treatise, he would be compelled to rearrange them, no doubt often clumsily, on his guitar, there not being a piano within many miles' radius of La Côte-Saint-André. When he first handled the former instrument is not quite certain. He apparently did not have real lessons until a musician named Dorant came to the village in July 1819 to teach Hector and his sister Nanci. The boy must have practised assiduously during the two years that elapsed before he departed for Paris, since his master declared his inability to instruct him further. In later years his powers of execution must have been considerable, if we may trust Legouvé's account of them.[1] The particular occasion was in 1833, when Berlioz was discussing his approaching marriage with Eugène Sue and Legouvé at the latter's rooms. His host having suggested some music, the composer.

'picked up his instrument and commenced to sing. What? Boleros, dance airs, melodies? Nothing of the kind? The finale to the second act of *La Vestale*! The chief priest, the vestals, Julia, he sang everything, all the characters, all the parts. Unhappily, he had no voice.[2] But that did not matter! He made one. Thanks to a system of singing *à bouche fermée*, which he practised with extraordinary skill, thanks to the passion and musical genius that inspired him, he drew from his chest, his throat and his guitar unknown sounds, penetrating lamentations, which, mingled at times with cries of admiration and enthusiasm, even eloquent commentaries, united to produce an effect so extraordinary, so incredible a whirlwind of brilliancy and passion that no performance of the masterpiece, even at the Conservatoire, has moved me, transported

---

[1] Op. cit.

[2] Barbier, on the other hand, says that Berlioz 'had a tenor voice and sang agreeably' (*Souvenirs personnels et silhouettes contemporaines*).

me so much as this singer without a voice and his guitar. After
La Vestale some fragments of the Fantastic Symphony.'

One wonders which those fragments were.

Without being a player on the instrument, it would
be presumption for me to dogmatize on the precise
manner in which the practice of the guitar may have
influenced Berlioz's musical thought. I can only suggest
tentatively that his partiality for chords in root position
had its origin in the greater resonance of the three lower
strings of the guitar—in the first inversion of common
chords the third would be apt to be too prominent.
That the thumb alone has to attend to these three
lower strings may possibly account for a certain stiffness
in his bass-line. It may also be the reason for his occasional method of writing several chords on the same
bass note, not in the manner of a pedal, but simply
because the note enters into all the chords. Since a
bare line of melody, or one only supported by occasional
chords, is a feature of guitar music, it might not be
wrong to connect it with some of the composer's
methods. The fact that, apart from the three lowest.
strings, which can give but a single note, there are
only three strings available for chords may have something to do with his partiality for triads.

Too much stress, however, must not be laid on
Berlioz's practice of the guitar. At the Conservatoire
he, like all the other students, would have had his ear
trained by means of the piano; and before that Gerono,
and afterwards Lesueur, would have illustrated the
chords on the instrument. He also learnt much from
his constant visits to the opera, either score in hand,
or after an intensive study of it. (When, on applying
for a post as chorister in a minor theatre, he reeled off
a list of operas he knew by heart, he was not exag-
gerating.) At home he would have continued to try
out combinations on the guitar; soon, however, he was
able to compose away from any instrument, as witness
his cantatas written to gain the *prix de Rome*. He may

have commenced his serious studies late in life, but
he brought to them the ability to read any music at
sight, and, though his employment of them was crude,
he had acquired the power of 'auralizing' the sound
of many chords. The fine Invocation in *Cleopatra* (1829)
owes nothing to the guitar; indeed the enharmonic
modulations smack somewhat of the keyboard.

The influence of the guitar on Berlioz's harmonic
ideas is probably infinitesimal, but, if I am right in
my suggestion, it may be sufficient to be vaguely
detected by those nurtured on a totally different
instrument. In any case it is undignified—not to use
a stronger word!—to impute so persistently to ignorance the ideas of a genius on harmony or anything else
simply because they do not chance to tally with our
own. Jomelli applied for a post in the Papal Chapel,
and the authorities agreed to accept him on condition
that he passed an examination. Jomelli consented to
the test, provided that he in his turn were allowed to
examine his examiners. His offer was declined. Probably, if the shade of Berlioz were permitted to examine
those who carp at him, they would find that he had
a very thorough knowledge of the rules of harmony—
the rules of 1830 *bien entendu*—from which his detractors had themselves deviated. M. Kœchlin, as regards
Berlioz's 'ignorance', says:[1]

'Sometimes they jeer at him in the class-rooms of the Conservatoire. Clever students, correct mediocrities, mock at what
they call his "false basses". It is easy to say this! But try, in
some bar of one of his melodies, what you believe to be the
"true bass"—a chord of the 6th, for example, instead of the
tonic which you find "clumsy", and you will see what a platitude it is. Do you really believe that, had he wanted it, he
was incapable of imagining this chord of the 6th, more in conformity with your petty scholastic ideas? If he has not done
so, he had good reason.'

M. Kœchlin gives here a simple example, but it illus-

[1] Op. cit.

trates the peculiar attitude of most of Berlioz's detractors. Do they really believe that he did not know rules
that the veriest dullard of a harmony class would learn
in a few weeks? The French theorist, like Schumann
ninety years ago, realizes that many of Berlioz's harmonic progressions lose their force, if they are 'corrected'. He says, speaking generally of the rules in
the text-books,

'there would have been many errors in musical history due to
this scholasticism, if real musicians throughout the centuries
had not treated the rules with a fair amount of freedom . . . if,
in the schools, they are useful, their importance must not be
exaggerated. . . . They [musicians] train the ear according to
the rules, and not according to their own sensibility (*propre sentiment*). There is the mistake: for it is the true musicality that we
must seek, that which *really satisfies our intimate feeling for music*.'

The insistence on the letter rather than the spirit
is, of course, to be found in all religions and in most
of the arts. It must be ascribed to the weakness or
timidity of its practitioners, though they themselves
define their attitude in very different terms. They
cling to the rock of some text or rule, fearful to trust
themselves to the open sea, where they would have to
be reliant on themselves, all unsuspecting that the rock
may break away or prove too slippery for their fingers.

For a non-technical and eminently common-sense
view of Berlioz's harmony, I would refer the reader
to Mr. Ernest Newman's *Musical Studies*. In the first
place, he points out, 'one needs scarcely any "training"
to avoid some of the progressions that Berlioz constantly uses'; secondly, that his earliest compositions
show less divergence from academic usage than his
later ones, which 'seems to show that his harmonic
style was rooted in his way of thinking, and became
more pronounced as he grew older and more individual'; thirdly, that 'if the peculiarities of his harmony
had been due to lack of education, one would have
expected him, when in more mature years he revised

an early work, to correct some of the so-called faults
to which a wider experience must have opened his
eyes'. Mr. Newman instances one of the songs, *Adieu,
Bessy*, composed in 1830, and revised in 1850, which
'he has altered in many ways, and made improvements in the melody, in the phrasing, and in the
accompaniment; but the sometimes odd harmonic
sequences of the original version remain unchanged in
the later. It clearly never struck him that there was
anything odd about them . . . it was a question not so
much of mere technique as of fundamental conception.'
Mr. Newman's 'fourthly' insists on the fact that
Berlioz thought in terms of the orchestra.

Some have suggested that Berlioz's harmony would
have been 'improved', had he been taught the piano
and been compelled to play the '48' of Bach for six
months on end. The suggestion is a curious one,
since it is equivalent to saying, 'We can't (or won't)
learn your language. But, if you will practise our
mode of expression, we may possibly understand you
more than we do at present.' Such of Bach's music
as Berlioz did hear, and it was very little, did not appeal
to him from the harmonic point of view. In 1840 he
heard an air from one of the 'Passions', and said in
his notice [1] that, while it possessed much of the 'antique
grief' that we find in Gluck, he 'was shocked by the
harmonic asperities and the false relations . . . the ear
is offended . . . and that is extremely painful, to say
the least of it !'

It is a commonplace that the radical of to-day is
the conservative of to-morrow. But as a rule the change
is only effected gradually and covers many years.
With Berlioz, however, the transformation was extra-
ordinarily rapid. Early in his career he made up his
mind on what harmonic methods best suited him,
and he clung tenaciously to them all his life, though

[1] I am indebted for my quotation to Boschot's *Un Romantique sous Louis-
Philippe*.

naturally employing them with greater mastery as he gained experience. Take, for example, his ideas on the appoggiatura. As Hippeau points out in *Berlioz et son temps*, while Wagner's system of harmony is based largely on its use, Berlioz seldom employs it. With the latter 'there is not a passing note that does not bear a harmony of its own, so that in fact, in this melodic structure, there is no passing note'. Like all generalities, this may not be the whole truth, but it is sufficiently near it for our purpose. In the *Journal des Débats* of 27 September 1835[1] he attacks the abuse of the appoggiatura in Hérold's *Zampa*, which 'de-naturalizes every chord, weakens the harshness of certain dissonances or augments it to the verge of discordance, transforms sweetness into insipidity, makes grace lackadaisical, and appears to me the most insufferable of the affectations of the Parisian school'. Twenty-five years later, he said of the prelude to *Tristan*: 'It is a slow piece, commencing pianissimo, gradually increasing to a fortissimo, and returning to the initial nuance, without any other theme than a sort of chromatic groan, but crowded with dissonant chords of which the long appoggiaturas replacing the real note of the harmony augment the cruelty.' This is from Berlioz's notice in the *Débats* of 9 February 1860 of the concerts that Wagner gave in Paris, and one wonders whether the German composer realized that his harmony was linked to that of the 'Parisian school' of the 1830's. Berlioz's criticism of the prelude was not based on mere audition; he had been able to study the score, since Wagner previous to his first concert had presented Berlioz with a full score of the complete opera, with the dedication: 'Au cher et grand auteur de *Roméo et Juliette*, l'auteur reconnaissant de *Tristan et Iseult*.' Without imputing ulterior motives to Wagner, it must be admitted that it was an

---

[2] Berlioz's article is reproduced in *Les Musiciens et la musique*, edited by André Hallays.

inauspicious moment to send such a gift to the leading musical critic of Paris. We may be sure that Marie Recio (then Madame Berlioz) lost no opportunity of pointing out the obvious bribery and corruption.

The copy of *Tristan* that Wagner gave to Berlioz is now in the Biblothèque Nationale at Paris, with the latter's comments scrawled on some fifty of its pages. I have not had a chance of inspecting it, but, thanks to the kindness of a friend, I possess Alfred Ernst's article dealing with the annotations.[1] An additional interest is attached to Ernst's remarks, since they display a struggle between his two loves—his early one for Berlioz and his more recent one for Wagner, whose genius he was one of the first in France to recognize. He strives to hold the balance truly, but at times seems inclined to support the German composer too eagerly. Thus, against Tristan's words in Act II, 'Uns're Liebe, Tristans Liebe' (*Min. Sc.*, p. 594), Berlioz wrote 'Agréable mélodie!!' On this Ernst remarks, 'This ironical comment is indeed singularly misplaced', and goes on to point out that the interval with which the phrase commences is only an inversion of the augmented 4th with which Berlioz begins *The King of Thule*. This, of course, is mere begging the question! He objected to the *whole* passage on pp. 594–5. It distressed him—and others in 1860—much as some of (say) Anton Webern's 'melodies' irritate many musicians of the present day.

When we remember that Berlioz evolved his own system of harmony in the 1830's, we can understand many of his strictures on that of Wagner. With his rooted objection to the appoggiatura, we can even understand his inability to appreciate the poignant beauty of the first chord in *Tristan*. At p. 141, bar 2 (*Min. Sc.*), the same chord appears, and he draws attention to the D♯ of the cor anglais against the F, B,

---

[1] 'Wagner corrigé par Berlioz', *Le Ménestrel*, 28 Sept. 1884. In the British Museum copies of the journal have been preserved only since 1885.

and G♯ of the bassoons and oboe.[1] There may be some
who share his annoyance at the sevenths between the
voices on pp. 626–7, and the violins and 'cellos on pp.
26–7. But, considering the discords penned by Berlioz
himself, one wonders why he was not more lenient as
regards some of Wagner's. As the former was a pioneer
in the employment of the unprepared chord of the 9th,
which in Beethoven's C minor symphony had excited
the ire of Fétis, and on occasion would use it in its
harshest form—with the 9th grinding against the root
in an upper part, one wonders why he did not appreciate the possibility of employing higher harmonics.
Yet we find him 'transported by fury' (to quote Alfred
Ernst) by the chord of the third bar of p. 321 (*Min. Sc.*)
of *Tristan*, taking the trouble to scrawl the offending
notes on the margin of the page—F♮, E♭, F♯, B♭, A
(counting upwards). With the F♯ correctly noted as
G♭, this 'strange chord' (to quote Ernst again) is
merely a chord of the 11th, with the 5th omitted.
We must remember, however, that, although all composers (including Berlioz himself) had employed combinations which are explained by Prout and others
as being derived from chords of the 11th and 13th,
the theorists of the time explained them—if they
explained them at all—in other ways. Even such a
composer as Saint-Saëns apparently did not admit the
chord of the 13th, if we may judge from an enigmati-
cal sentence in his *École buissonnière*. Having remarked
that Offenbach has had the audacity to write an unprepared chord of the 11th in *Daphnis et Chloé* (1860),
he goes on to explain dominant discords, and how
they are built up by adding thirds. Having arrived
at a chord of the 11th, he proceeds: 'After that we
can do nothing: a third more, and we come to the

---

[1] Berlioz evidently took the real chord to be that of the diminished 7th
on G♯. But, as with many of these ' altered chords ', another interpretation
is possible. We may consider the chord as that of the augmented 6th, with
the A altered, resolving on dominant harmony.

fundamental note, at a distance of two octaves.' This, of course, is contrary to fact!

At the commencement of Act i, Scene 3, Berlioz scribbled 'Horreurs!' against the ascending scale of the violins opposed to the descending one of the basses, and with this we may leave his 'corrections' of Wagner. He was more irritated with his contemporary than he had been with Beethoven, but one has only to read his analyses of the symphonies of the Bonn master to realize that at times he was inclined to shake his head over some of his idol's harmonic methods. He was, for example, utterly unable to perceive any reason for the crash of all the notes of the minor scale (chord of the 13th) in the Ninth Symphony. Yet he must have been dimly conscious of such a chord. The juxtaposition of the major triad on D♭ and the minor one on G, in the March to Execution, can partly be explained by regarding both chords as consisting of upper partials of C. It is to be noted that, if we may trust the negative evidence of Ernst's article, Berlioz passed no comments on Wagner's orchestration, though certain passages, such as the excessive division of the strings in Act ii, are open to criticism, and, as the composer admitted to Levi in later years,[1] portions of the Love Duet are too heavily scored. Berlioz confined his strictures to the harmony, and, when dealing with Beethoven's symphonies, he touches more often on the harmony than the instrumentation. We can find other instances of the interest he took in the former throughout his life. Whatever opinion may be held as to the French master's own harmonic methods, there can be no doubt that they did not result from either ignorance or chance. He had reasoned out his own particular system quite as thoroughly as his detractors have theirs. Possibly more so, for, while they are disposed to accept the teachings of their text-books, his musical instinct led him to question many things he was taught at the

[1] See Appendix to Kufferath's *Tristan et Iseult*.

Conservatoire, and to justify his objections. There are iconoclasts who would destroy without having formulated any ideas as to what should replace that which they would tear down. To call a creative artist one of these is a contradistinction in terms.

Intelligent amateurs, admirers of Berlioz, who think for themselves, must often wonder at some of the denunciations of the master's harmonic methods. Their ears tell them that he at times employs chords and progressions such as Mendelssohn would not have used, but do not Ravel, Stravinsky, Mussorgsky, and many other modern men do likewise? Wherein lies the difference? And the wonder naturally becomes greater when the authorities disagree. We have an eminent musician declaring that the opening chords of the Invocation to Nature remind him of 'an adventurous harmony-pupil let loose for the first time amongst the joys of diminished triads and augmented sixths'. On the other hand, we find M. Kœchlin in 'Le Cas Berlioz'[1] citing these same chords, 'with the beautiful enharmonic modulations' as one of the proofs that the French master was 'an infinitely greater harmonist than his detractors imagine'. To M. Marnold[2] those same modulations are 'wearisome and sterile', and he, as a well-known musical critic and the author of some books on musical theory, is entitled to consideration. He receives less because he spoils his own case by his too sweeping condemnation of Berlioz's music. We have authority for believing that 'you can fool some of the people all the time', but when that time extends over a century and 'some of the people' include 'many competent and sensitive judges (critics, practising musicians of all orders, and plain listeners) who have never felt any poverty or clumsiness in Berlioz's music',[3] there is reason to doubt the truth of the dictum.

---

[1] *La Revue musicale*, Feb. 1922.   [2] Op. cit.
[3] 'Berlioz: A Postscript to a Discussion', *The Musical Times*, April 1929, by M. D. Calvocoressi.

It would seem that to obtain a true idea of Berlioz's merits as a harmonist, we should for the time being drop him out of the discussion, and confine our attention to arguing about the relative merits of his admirers and opponents, not from the point of view of academic distinction, but rather from that of broad-mindedness and the power to find truth and beauty in a work of art, even though it be framed on principles different from one's own. In fact, the attitude of Berlioz's critics, whatever may be the conclusions at which they arrive, should be the precise contrary of his own bigoted one.

In having very pronounced ideas on what was right in technique, Berlioz did not differ greatly from other composers. One who veered with every wind that blew would not achieve much. As his style remained unchanged, there was no particular reason why he should materially alter his medium of expression. *The Damnation of Faust* (1845) might have been composed seventeen or eighteen years before. In fact, eight of the numbers had already appeared in *Eight Scenes from Faust* (1829), and in all probability the Ride to the Abyss and the Pandæmonium date back to 1828, when he was setting music to the contemplated Faust ballet. That the first scene, Faust's meditation, and his Invocation to Nature would have been as they are now could not be expected. In his younger days he naturally had not the same command of his armoury, and did not possess maturity of thought. But, as regards style, there is as little clash between the earlier and the later work as there is between Mendelssohn's overture to *A Midsummer's Night's Dream* and the numbers he added in after years. I would add that the idea that the music of the *Eight Scenes* was incorporated in its pristine form in the later work is totally wrong. A collation of the two versions of the Easter Hymn alone is sufficient to dispel that belief. And as many of the alterations concerned the harmony, it would be of interest to know what his detractors consider guided

Berlioz when he altered that of his early works. As
they would appear to deny him any carefully thought-
out system by which he judgèd his own and others'
harmony, it must have been a case of the blind leading
the blind. It is to be regretted that he did not obtain
that professorship at the Conservatoire he sought. He
might have written a treatise on harmony. It would
now be as obsolete as that of Fétis, but would at any
rate show that he possessed very definite ideas on the
subject.

To admirers of Berlioz some of the objections to
his harmony are incomprehensible, as difficult to appreciate as those which he advanced against the harmony
of Wagner or Liszt. I would instance one of them,
since it bears on the orchestral nature of a great deal
of his own harmony. The third bar of his wonderful
song *Absence* has been censured, and would seem to
have offended some ears so much that their owners
are incapable of realizing the beauty of the piece.
Here are the opening bars, as they stand in the piano
version, the parts for both hands being crowded on to
one staff.

Berlioz's 'crime' is that he failed to resolve the chord B–C♯–E♯ (last inversion of the chord of the dominant 7th) according to the text-books. Following them, the bass of the next chord should be A♯ instead of F♯. Here, perhaps, we have an illustration of Berlioz being 'more of an artist than a musician'. The mere musician might have written the A♯, and been guilty of 'a platitude of an insufferable banality and finicality (*mièvrerie*)', to quote M. Kœchlin: the artist realized the weakness of repeating the opening phrase in mutilated form. Even from the piano version I fancy that an unbiased listener would agree with the French theorist. In the orchestral setting the composer's intentions become clearer. Only a few instruments are required for the song—2 flutes, 1 oboe, 2 clarinets, 2 horns, and a small number of strings.[1] To those with ears to hear, the tritone B–E♯ is unmistakably resolved according to the rules, the upper note (on the voice) going to F♯ and the lower on the oboe and second clarinet going to A♯. That the other instruments break in with the initial phrase does not obscure the resolution. Berlioz did not consider his chords on the orchestra as merely chunks of harmony, as on a piano: each section of the orchestra had an independent existence. As Mr. Ernest Newman has put it, he treated the different instruments as though they were on different planes, a method practised in many modern scores, which permits concatenations of notes of atrocious effect on a piano, and such vagaries as the synchronous employment of two keys.

The difficulty experienced by so many as regards the appreciation of Berlioz's harmony arises from two causes. First, because his ideas, in the words of Dr. Percy Buck,[2] have never become 'current coinage'.

[1] There is a facsimile of the opening bars of *Absence* in Julius Kapp's *Berlioz*, with a memorandum by the composer as to how many parts would require copying. Besides those for the wind instruments he wanted 4 for the first violins, 4 for the second, 3 for the violas, and 5 for the basses.

[2] At the Berlioz Conference, held in Dec. 1928.

The reason for this is without doubt because he has had no *direct* imitators. I shall return to this question in my last chapter. Secondly, because although Berlioz used enharmony, with rare exceptions it is not the enharmony that is cultivated by other musicians, which is based on keyboard practice. Saint-Saëns[1] gives us some lucid remarks on this point. He asks:

'Who, in our time, has not submitted to the powerful influence of the piano? This influence which began before the piano itself with the "Das wohltemperierte Klavier" of Sebastian Bach. From the day when the *temperament* of the chord led to the synonymity of sharps and flats and allowed the practice of all tonalities, the spirit of the keyboard entered into the world: this spirit has become the devastating tyrant of music by the excessive propagation of the heretical[2] enharmony. From this heresy has sprung almost all modern art: it has been too fertile to give us cause to deplore it, but it is none the less a heresy destined to disappear in the future, probably far distant, but inevitable, as the result of the same evolution that gave it birth. What then will remain of present-day art? Perhaps only that of Berlioz, who, never having learnt the piano, had an instinctive objection to enharmony.'

[1] *Portraits et souvenirs*, article on Franz Liszt.
[2] 'Heretical', since it is illogical that a choir or a string quartet should be treated as keyboard instruments.

Chapter Four

MELODY, FORM, AND PROGRAMMES

As with Berlioz's harmony, so with his melody. In attempting to discuss it, we are confronted by a number of competent authorities who flatly contradict one another. We have Dr. Weingartner [1] telling us that, after it had been impressed upon him that the French master had no melody, he read the overture to *Benvenuto Cellini*, and was filled with delighted astonishment as melody after melody was unfolded before his eyes until he had discovered 'five grand themes, all plastic, original, of admirable workmanship, varied in form, and rising gradually to a culminating point to finish with intense effect'. Sir Thomas Beecham [2] declares that *The Damnation of Faust* contains 'a bunch of the loveliest tunes in existence'. One would have thought that these two musicians, both men of eclectic tastes and conductors of wide experience, could be trusted to know what they are talking about. But no! We have musicians, equally competent, although, of course, obviously more narrow-minded in their musical tastes, who insist that Berlioz was incapable of writing a melody; and we are told, as though it were a statement of fact, such things as that 'no musician could approve the cor anglais melody of *The Roman Carnival* Overture'. Mr. Stewart Macpherson —scarcely to be dismissed as no musician—however, [3] after having given a number of examples of melodies, in which 'the second phrase responds to the first, not only in *rhythmic shape*, but also in *melodic pattern*' goes on to say that 'unity is often preserved merely by the general tenor of the passage, by which we are made to feel that its various "limbs" are in keeping one with

---

[1] *Le Guide musical*, 29 Nov. 1903.
[2] *The Daily Telegraph*, 27 May 1933.
[3] *Form in Music*, London, 1915.

another, although varied in outline'. As a 'good example' of this he quotes the cor anglais melody !

It is to be regretted that Berlioz's detractors—or, for the matter of that, his admirers—have not given us a definition of what they mean by melody. Those in the text-books range from Prout's 'sounds of different pitch heard one after another' to 'something that can be whistled'. Admitting that as regards whistling the powers of execution of the ordinary musician yield to those of many a street arab, still, if the former cannot reproduce with pursed lips in recognizable form any one of some half-hundred of Berlioz's tunes after once hearing it, there must be something lacking in him. The fundamental reason, however, why Berlioz's melodies are not approved of by his detractors is because they do not possess a particular *form*, which appears to depend principally on repetition, either of phrase, rhythm, or pattern. The expressiveness of a melody seems to count for little, and, in vocal music, a faithful translation of the words to be of no great import. Mr. Bernard Shaw[1] suggests that if Charles Lecocq had set *La ci darem la mano*, he would have 'simply composed the first line and the fourth, and then repeated them without altering a note. In the sixties and seventies nobody minded this. . . . It not only saved the composer the trouble of composing : it was positively popular ; for it made the tunes easier to learn. Besides, I need hardly say that there are all sorts of precedents, from *The Vicar of Bray* to the finale of Beethoven's choral symphony, to countenance it.' Unfortunately, what nobody minded seventy years ago has become an article of faith to many, possibly because their belief goes with their convenience—it makes composition easier. It requires a greater gift for melodic invention to compose the 'masterly theme of twenty-three bars' which Weingartner found early in the *Cellini* overture, than to compose four bars, and then

[1] *Music in London, 1890–94*, vol. iii, p. 36.

to hammer out four others to match them. Fine tunes have been created on this symmetrical principle, but to insist that it is the only one possible seems a negation of art.

Whatever may be the correct definition of melody, supposing it to be definable at all, few would question that it is the essential part of music. Chord progressions may be highly effective for a short time, but even with them the composer usually seeks to make the separate parts of some melodic interest. Admirers of Schubert's music base their admiration on appreciation of his melodiousness : those who profess to find no melody in Berlioz have no liking for his music. Their position is reasonable. If they insist that the opening phrase of *The Damnation of Faust* is not a melody, how can they admire the first scene, which is a development of it ? As Berlioz felt music as few have ever done, it is only to be expected that his ideas of melody should differ largely from those of (say) Auber, who ought logically to hold a high place in the affections of many musicians, for his sprightly tunes certainly conform to what they apparently seek in melody. M. Masson,[1] having insisted on the 'originality, the abundance, and the variety, which have rarely been surpassed in the history of music,' of Berlioz's melody, proceeds :

'It moulds itself to every expression, lends itself to all the exigences of the poetic idea, marries the most opposite characters with an astonishing sureness and mobility. In it Berlioz displays to the full his essentially dramatic genius, and so to speak his gifts as an actor in music, his instinctive ability to mimic by melody the most diverse sentiments. . . . It is literally a gesture in sound (*geste sonore*).'

As an excellent example of how closely Berlioz can depict a character in music, take the four-bar melody for the first violins and 'cellos shortly after Marguerite's entrance in *The Damnation of Faust*:

[1] *Les Maîtres de la musique—Berlioz*, Paris, 1923.

Ex. 2.

It follows immediately on her words *mon futur amant*
—the damsel was evidently prepared to meet Faust
half-way—when she is recalling her dream of the
previous night. As a melody it verges on the commonplace and the *gruppetto* at the end is almost vulgar.
But does it not admirably portray the Gretchen of
Goethe's *Faust*, in which, readers will remember, the
girl herself lays stress on her lowly condition, on her
hands red and coarsened by toil? Marguerite sings
the melody at the end of her Romance, when she recalls Faust's bearing and gestures, and the music
continues in the same strain until we come to her
hysterical outburst, which is most assuredly not the
grief of a *grande dame*. The poor forsaken girl here
probably reverted to type and threw her apron over
her head. Berlioz has given us a faithful portrait of a
young woman of low degree loved by a fine gentleman.
If Marguerite had confided in a female friend, she
would certainly have described her lover in verbal
language corresponding to our example, *gruppetto* included. In the language of the penny novelette, she
was a poor girl with nothing but her love, and, to
illustrate that love, the composer, after the hysterical
outburst, puts into her mouth one of the most magnificent passages ever given to a singer. Incidentally,
this wonderful musical picture occurs in the *Eight
Scenes from Faust*, Berlioz's original Opus 1!

Some apologists for the composer endeavour to explain him by insisting that it is impossible to appreciate him properly unless we take into consideration
the 'literary element' in him. Possibly the above
remarks on Marguerite's music may be taken as an
illustration of it. They were not so intended. Berlioz
was an educated man and, as with every other artist,

no matter what his medium of expression, he betrays this in his music; and, as he says in his definition of music in *A travers chants*, he considered the art to be one for *hommes intelligents*. It does not, however, require much intelligence or pronounced literary tastes to realize that most of the ladies with beautifully manicured hands, who appear in Gounod's opera, do not resemble the Gretchen of Goethe. And if in dramatic music a musician demands nothing more than a pleasing melody to represent this or that character, quite irrespective of whether it portrays it truthfully, it is scarcely a commendable attitude.

Saint-Saëns declared Berlioz to be 'more of an artist than a musician', and M. Masson and others have repeated the remark without perhaps realizing all its implications. Leaving for the moment the question of melody, is it not strange that we had to wait for an *artist* amongst composers to perceive the absurdity, the irreverence, of making fugues on the word Amen? And this fugal absurdity was not confined to a single word. Mr. Bernard Shaw,[1] speaking of *Israel in Egypt*, says: 'Berlioz's burlesque *Amen* is far less laughable than *He led them through the deep as through a wilderness*, the insane contrapuntal vagaries of the four last words surpassing in irreverent grotesqueness anything that the boldest buffoon dare offer as a professedly comic composition.' The passage might be matched by many others in the works of those who without doubt were musicians, but whose artistic perceptions were obviously uncultivated. Indeed, the word 'artist' as applied to a musician is of recent usage. Adolphe Adam, writing in 1834 on 'The Musicians of Paris',[2] records the fact that to the majority of people the word connotes a painter. As Berlioz admitted the repetition of words on other occasions, he could not logically object to that of Amen—in moderation. As he said to the Abbé

[1] Op. cit.
[2] Included in his *Souvenirs d'un musicien*, Paris, 1857.

Girod:[1] 'No doubt it would be possible to write a beautiful fugue to express the pious wish *Amen*. But it would have to be slow, full of contrition, and very short; for however well the sense of a word may be expressed, that word cannot be repeated a great number of times without its becoming ridiculous.' Is there any musician living at the present time who would seriously dispute Berlioz's statement? His objection was to the traditional fugue on the word *Amen*, which he stigmatizes as being 'rapid, violent, turbulent, resembling nothing more than some chorus of drinkers mingled with peals of laughter, as each part vocalizes on the first syllable of the *a . . . a-a-a-amen*, producing a most grotesque and indecent effect'. He even had the courage to criticize Beethoven himself on this point. That Berlioz was particularly enamoured of the fugue as a form of composition cannot be pretended. Somewhere he describes it as the tiresome repetition of a meaningless phrase, or in words to that effect. But he had certainly no objection to the fugato, which he employs sixteen times or more, on occasion achieving a recognizable fugue, if a free one, and even a double one, as with the *Sabbat* and the first number of the *Te Deum*. Except as evidence of Berlioz's artistic perceptions, his ideas on fugue have no more interest than those of Chopin on double counterpoint. Cherubini, having, as head of the Conservatoire, passed Berlioz four times as being competent to write fugue, delivered himself of the epigram that his erstwhile student 'did not like fugue, because the fugue did not like him'. Against that may be set the opinion of Ebenezer Prout, who, in whatever esteem he may be held by the present generation, was certainly a first-rate authority on the principles of fugue composition, that 'the fugued "Hosanna" proves that, whatever may have been the causes of Berlioz's antipathy to fugues in general, inability to compose in that style was

[1] *Correspondance inédite*, Letter LXXXIII.

certainly not one of them'.[1] The eminent theorist and critic, of course, knew nothing of the two fugues which have since appeared in the German edition, uninspired student fugues, if you will—it is difficult to imagine Berlioz inspired by any set dry academic theme!—but sufficient to prove that Cherubini was justified in passing him.

The cliché of Berlioz not liking fugue is only part of the general accusation brought against him, that he had no sense of form, either in melody or in his symphonic movements. In the latter case he is sometimes grudgingly excused by the suggestion that he dislocated the more or less consecrated form on account of his programme or this mysterious 'literary element'. As regards his melody, there is no logical reason why he should have adopted a form founded on repetition. Without driving Masson's simile too hard, cannot a *geste sonore* be graceful, beautiful, expressive without being in any way dependent on the symmetry of repetition? An arresting gesture with the right hand need not be immediately followed by a similar one with the left, in the pump-handle style of an Italian tenor. Indeed, the significance of a gesture may be accentuated if it be succeeded by one that, taken by itself, might almost belie it. Taking melody to be the expression of some emotion, there does not appear to be any powerful reason why an emotion should be cut up into four-bar lengths, like a string of sausages, though no doubt they may be very succulent. Melody may have been evolved from the association of music with metrical compositions, but there would seem to be no reason why the rules that govern the latter should apply to the former. To compare some 'irregularity' in one of Berlioz's melodies as being equivalent to a false quantity in an hexameter is a confusion of ideas. He was not writing hexameters, he was writing music.

[1] *The Athenaeum*, 2 June 1887.

Berlioz's tunes need no apology. That they are not approved by every one is understandable. All those of other composers are not approved by admirers of the French master, or even by the professed admirers of the other composers. In testing Berlioz's melodies, and objecting to them because they do not comply with some particular species of form, his opponents leave out of account his wonderful rhythms, the pulsation of which makes an organic whole of even his longest phrases. Take, for example, that for the bassoons at the commencement of the Soldiers' Chorus, based roughly on a descending scale through two octaves. It is a phrase of nine bars, and therefore presumably non-compliant with some imaginary rule that melodies should consist of phrases of two bars or some multiple of it. As Mr. Stewart Macpherson says :[1] 'Phrases of five, six, and seven bars are occasionally met with, but they are of comparatively infrequent occurrence.' Exactly! Without for a moment disparaging the fine melodies that have been constructed on that principle, it may be pointed out that they have had their origin in a peculiarity of the human ear. A clock ticks perfectly evenly, and yet to the ordinary man it sounds in duple rhythm—*tick*-tock. One needs to be somewhat of a musician to hear it tick in threes or fives. And here we have an astounding thing! The objection to Berlioz's phrases of an uneven number of bars is principally confined to musicians, who, it would be supposed, would welcome melodies that broke away from the methods practised in cabaret tunes. Berlioz endeavoured to express more by his melodies than many composers, but I do not fancy he often wrote them with any ulterior motive. That is, he did not mould his subjects in a symphonic movement with an eye to their development in the German style. When he attempts that style, he is not always successful. He had his own methods of development, and to those who

[1] Op. cit.

can view music *as* music without reference to that of other composers, those methods are of great interest.

Paradoxically, some minds seem to move more freely in fetters, either of their own contriving or previously utilized by others. Some poets, for instance, appear to produce their best work when employing some rigid form of verse such as that of the sonnet. The fact of being relieved of finding the correct form to fit their ideas assists the flow of them. And many of their readers, having carefully counted the lines and noted the rhymes, will accept the sonnet without troubling whether after all that form was the best suited for the expression of the content. In any work of art there should be a perfect correlation between the thought and its presentation; and only by this can true form be achieved. As Berlioz said in 1853, when working on *The Trojans*: 'The immense difficulty as regards it, is to find the musical *form*, that form without which music does not exist, or is no more than the humble slave of the word.'[1] Later on in the letter: 'To find the means of being *expressive*, *true*, without ceasing to be a musician, and on the other hand to give to the music new qualities, that is the problem.' These are hardly the remarks of a man who indulged in a 'fortuitous concourse of phrases, without form and void'.

Without possessing the rigidity of the sonnet form, in music the sonata form might be compared with it. Similarly, many listeners will accept the latter form without troubling to decide whether the content of the movement is best expressed in it, or whether some modification might not be advisable, such as the second subject preceding instead of following the first one in the recapitulation section.[2] We talk of

---

[1] *Briefe von Hector Berlioz an die Fürstin Carolyne Sayn-Wittgenstein*, edited by La Mara, Leipzig, 1903, Letter XI. The sentence quoted contains a misprint—*sous laquelle* for *sans laquelle*.

[2] Stewart Macpherson cites examples from Mozart, Spohr, and Dvořák where this has been done.

Beethoven enlarging the sonata form. But there is another way of looking at the matter. His elaboration of the coda, the introduction of important episodes, the employment of a theme of the introduction into the working-out section, and the like, may be regarded as attempts to escape from the fetters of the form, just as the additional two lines to the sonnets in Meredith's *Modern Love* may be viewed in two lights. The question might be argued at length, but all that concerns us here is the absurdity of the idea that, because a poetical, musical, or architectural work deviates from some previous form, therefore it must needs be formless. As we have seen, Berlioz, having conceived an idea, cast around for the best form to fit it, 'that form without which music does not exist'. That he was invariably successful in his choice no one would pretend, but his plan had one inestimable advantage—it saved him from the temptation of indulging in padding. Even in the greatest of symphonic works we at times find passages where the composer has sacrificed on the altar of the Moloch of Form. It is true that those passages often exhibit technical skill, but that does not entirely atone for them. Those who profess to be satisfied with mere cleverness soon tire of it, as witness their opinion of some works by minor composers which, as regards technique, would put many of Beethoven's in the shade.

When seeking a form wherein to express himself, Berlioz was always inclined to turn to classic models. His first introduction to music was by way of Haydn's quartets and those of Pleyel, who sought to rival him. And by nature, in spite of his innovations, he was more conservative than revolutionary. He certainly never aimed at creating a 'new art', as Wagner unwisely asserted on one occasion. In 1830, in a letter to his sister Nanci, he exclaimed : 'When I dream of that field of chords which scholastic prejudices have until now preserved intact, and, since my emancipation, I reɜard as my domain, I rush forward in a kind of frenzy to explore it.' With harmony, he might have included form and melody, in which he saw possibilities neglected by scholastic prejudice—that of Paris in the 1820's we must not forget. Ignorant of Bach, Mozart, and Beethoven, he did not realize that some of the fields he deemed unexplored had been already tilled. The fact that he rediscovered those fields may not increase the merit of his scores, but it should make us realize the wonder of him as a musician. To credit him with having invented the symphonic poem is erroneous. In the Fantastic Symphony he showed how a theme representing an idea, an *idée fixe* he calls it, could be modified in accordance with its surroundings; in the *Harold in Italy* Symphony he illustrated the opposite—a theme unaffected by its environment. The method in the earlier symphony appealed to Liszt. He elaborated it, and hence arose the symphonic poem, of which the main characteristic is that the several sections are based on permutations of one or other of the representative themes. Berlioz's nearest approach to this plan is in *The Captive*. In the Fantastic Symphony the sole example of the method is the burlesque of the *idée fixe* in the last movement. It is obviously tacked on to the March; it might be cut out of the Waltz without injury to the form of the number; the concluding bars of the *Sabbat* recall it; it enters more intimately into the slow movement, but that was practically rewritten after the first performance, and therefore the *idée fixe* was more deeply embedded in the music—it was not added to a piece otherwise complete. In the death scene in *Romeo and Juliet* we find a metamorphosis of the Love Theme; and in numerous other places, partly owing to his method of development and partly to preserve unity, there are permutations of some theme which may be taken as representative of some character or idea.

Berlioz's scores are rich in suggestions for any maker

of symphonic poems, but he did not create the thing itself, principally perhaps because his ideas on 'programme music' differed considerably from those of Liszt or Richard Strauss. Before attempting to define those of the older master, I would quote an admirable passage by a modern critic[1] on what 'programme music' ought to be. It occurs in an article on Strauss:

'"Programme music", in its original shape, never loses its essentially musical basis of thought, and it reacts only to needs which are at the bottom those of all romantic imagery. Imagination—the concept of exterior things—becomes so vivid that it permeates the mind of the composer with the reality of its conception, and thus permeates his music. Thus the music becomes to some extent a function of the imaginative faculty, but it never loses its natural rhythm, as marked as the natural rhythm of speech or thought. Musical and dramatic imagery must retain an equipoise—as in Berlioz, and more than in Liszt.'

I do not know in what estimation Signor Pannain holds Berlioz, but as regards the equipoise between the music and the imagery he is indubitably correct. It exists, I believe, because Berlioz was less of a follower of programmes and more of a musician pure and simple than is generally supposed. He may have found a programme a stimulus to composition, and set out to illustrate it. But if it conflicted with his musical ideas he was always ready to disregard it, or rather, he was always prepared to give a very free rendering of it. An equipoise between a translation and the original is not best obtained by reproducing the idioms peculiar to the latter. He was as averse from making music the 'humble slave' of an idea as that of the words of a poem. Obsessed by the notion that Berlioz was unable to compose without a definite programme constantly in his mind, commentators have sought to explain his music in terms of one, when a purely musical reason

[1] *Modern Composers,* by Guido Pannain, translated by Michael R. Bonavia, London, 1932.

would suffice. As an example of this, take a criticism of the little violin piece of 1839, *Rêverie et Caprice*: 'Turn to the title-page and you find that everything has an inner meaning, that the F-sharp minor implies despair, that a semiquaver figure is meant to symbolize doubt or agitation, and that "voluptés fougueuses" are embodied in a most innocent-looking melody.' The cream of the jest is that Berlioz did not pen the non-sensical farrago that heads the score in the second French edition, as any one with any understanding of the composer might have guessed. It does not appear on the edition published in his lifetime, and was added after a Berlioz concert on 26 March 1880, when Marie Tayau played the solo part. It was written by M. Tiersot (then aged twenty) at the instigation of Pasdeloup, who, although he gave good interpretations of the master, was sufficient of a fogey to believe that a programme was a necessity for Berlioz.[1] (Fogeyism, the clinging to obsolete ideas, is usually associated with elderly gentlemen, but the failing can be discovered in the young, when it is more dangerous, since it is unsuspected.) The nonsense is reproduced in the untrustworthy German edition (vol. vi), but the commentary dealing with the work is discreetly silent on the point.

Even Wagner, when discussing Berlioz's music, fell into the error of connecting it with a non-existent programme. In criticizing the *Romeo and Juliet* Symphony with his friends,[2] he said:

'In instrumental music I am a *réactionnaire*, a conservative. I dislike everything that requires a verbal explanation beyond the actual sounds. For instance, the middle of Berlioz's touching *scène d'amour* in his "Romeo and Juliet" is meant by him to reproduce the lines about the lark and the nightingale in

---

[1] M. Tiersot nobly acknowledges his youthful error in 'Berlioziana', *Le Ménestrel*, 5 Nov. 1905.

[2] *Die Musik und ihre Classiker in Aussprüchen Richard Wagners*, Leipzig, 1876. Extracts given in *Grove's Dictionary*, art. 'Wagner'.

Shakespeare's balcony scene, but it does nothing of the sort—
it is not intelligible as music.'

Wagner found the opening of the Love Scene 'heav-
enly', and I do not suppose he troubled to visualize the
garden, the balcony, or even the protagonists. He
listened as he would to an Adagio of Beethoven's.
That is, he thought musically. Then comes the Allegro
agitato, and here the German was unable to follow the
Frenchman's *musical* idea, so he needs must invent
an imaginary programme, and then accuse Berlioz of
having failed to illustrate it. *The lines about the lark and
the nightingale do not occur in the balcony scene!* Wagner
in his stricture must be classed with the previous
writer I have quoted, and was not far removed from
the lady, who to Berlioz's amusement, discovered in
the Ball Scene Romeo arriving in his cabriolet.

What Berlioz precisely intended by his Allegro
agitato I do not venture to affirm—probably a picture
of Juliet on her balcony confiding her love to the night.
Musically, it is quite intelligible. The figure

Ex. 3.

is a legitimate development of the violin flutter

of the preceding Adagio. It can be paralleled in many
of his scores. In his first instrumental work, the overture to *Les Francs Juges*, he commences the introduction
with a phrase vaguely suggestive of the first subject
of the Allegro, and this is developed for a score of bars
until we come to the majestic theme for brass—at the
time an absolutely novel proceeding. At its termination
there is a crash for full orchestra (*coup de poignard*,
Berlioz calls it) succeeded by three crotchet thirds on
the oboes and violas descending chromatically ($\downarrow = 72$).

In the Allegro we find again the melody of the introduction, and the three chromatic notes, which might
almost have escaped notice, thundered out in semi-
breves (o= 80, wrongly given in the German edition
as d= 80) on the trombones with terrific effect. As
at the time Berlioz wrote the overture he knew no
more of Beethoven than some Andante, he did not
derive the idea of introducing material from the introduction into the succeeding Allegro from the Bonn
master. He evolved it himself, and made use of it in all
his overtures, with the exception of *Waverley*, where
the motto that heads the score

> Dreams of Love and lady's charms
> Give place to honour and to arms

necessitates a sharp distinction between the love theme
of the introduction and the warlike ones of the Allegro.
In the overture to *Beatrice and Benedick* it is true we
do not have the plan, but the second subject (a phrase
taken from the Wedding March) is sufficiently like
the air of the introductory Andante (Beatrice's air in
Act ii), on account of both commencing with a descending chromatic scale of four notes, to lead a careful
critic and an admirer of Berlioz[1] to imagine that the
two were identical. Incidentally, he considered the work
to be the weakest of Berlioz's overtures. A rather odd
opinion, since it chances to be one of the few pieces
of the French master that his opponents seem to
appreciate. Yet it is true Berlioz throughout!

The utilization of the theme of the introduction in
the subsequent Allegro may at times have had some
dramatic significance, as in *Les Francs Juges*. At others,
there would seem to be no reason except a musical
one, a desire to impart unity to a composition. In *The
Roman Carnival* Overture, as Teresa and Cellini were
present at the Carnival, from a programme point of
view it is fitting that their love music should figure in

---

[1] Richard Pohl, *Hector Berlioz: Studien und Erinnerungen*, Leipzig,
1884.

the midst of the general merriment, but it is difficult
to find a 'literary element' in its humorous treatment.
The relative importance of the three themes of the
work is—the second subject of the Allegro, the Love
Theme of the introduction, the first subject of the
Allegro, which might be taken to represent, with its
rhythm of a saltarello, the atmosphere of the Carnival
rather than anything more definite. With this in
mind, Gustav Brecher, in an excellent analysis of the
work,[1] is inclined to treat the overture as a sort of
symphonic poem. In this he errs. On the other hand,
the anonymous compiler of the Synopsis of Form in
the Philharmonia edition of the score, striving to bring
the work into line with the classical sonata form, has
completely misunderstood the composer's intentions.
He says that the first subject (interrupted by an Andante
—bars 19 to 78) extends from bar 1 to bar 127, when
the subsidiary subject begins (bars 128 to 167) 'chiefly
based on motives taken from the Principal Subject',
the Recapitulation following immediately on bar 168,
followed by a long Coda (bar 300). What Berlioz really
did was this: he took from the Carnival Scene of
Benvenuto Cellini his first and second subjects—indeed,
as the opera now stands, the first 169 bars of the main
Allegro of the overture are practically the same as those
of the Scene, naturally with different orchestration
(since the voice parts are eliminated) and with a few
changes in the harmony.[2] Anxious to foreshadow the
coming Allegro by a few bars of it previous to the
Andante—a plan he employed in other works—and
realizing that his second subject was considerably
stronger than his first one, he chose a few bars of
the former, which he was forced to transpose into the
key of the overture (A major). His proceeding was

[1] *Musikführer*, No. 175, 'Le Carnaval romain', Leipzig.

[2] What he absolutely did apparently was to make some alterations in the
saltarello (then in 3/4 time) as it stood in the original version of the opera,
and then transfer those alterations back to the Carnival Scene, when he
recast *Benvenuto Cellini*.

perfectly logical and perfectly understandable, although
it did appear to be beyond the comprehension of the
anonymous compiler. He, with distorted notions as
to what constitutes 'form', was prepared to label anything that came *first* as a 'first subject',[1] even though
it involved making the second subject identical with
it. There is no need to query the remainder of the
Philharmonia synopsis beyond pointing out that what
its author takes to be the Recapitulation is simply the
Exposition repeated (with different orchestration and
some minor variations), a procedure common enough
in the sonata form, but less practised in the modified
one usually employed in overtures. There is a short
development, and the Recapitulation does not include
the first subject (an omission found in the works of
other composers) because we have had already the
rhythm of it. Again Berlioz is perfectly logical! His
conservatism impelled him to cling to a classical model:
his radicalism led him to modify it in accordance with
the musical content of his score. Had his first subject
been stronger than the second, his treatment of his
material would have been different. To argue that he
ought to have chosen a stronger first subject, that he
ought not to have commenced his work with an arresting phrase from the second subject—in short, that he
ought to have moulded his ideas to fit a form invented
by Italians and developed by Germans, is beside the
point.

As an example of a work more closely attached to
some vague programme, let us take the overture to
King Lear. Without presuming to possess the ability
to penetrate into Berlioz's mental processes, I can
imagine him setting out to illustrate the initial idea
of the play—Lear's division of his kingdom. He may

[1] His attitude was paralleled by that of a writer of the programme of a
B.B.C. concert, in which we were told that the rushing scales that commence *The Corsair* Overture, afterwards used as transitional passages, were
the *first subject* of the work!

have done so merely to have an excuse for introducing a melody depicting Cordelia. In any case, he commences with a theme on the basses undoubtedly representative of Lear, answered by the muted violins in the octave above, as though he had questioned Goneril and she had returned the precise answer he had expected. He then turns to Regan with the complementary half of his theme, and receives the anticipated 'glib and oily' reply. He does not question Cordelia, because for musical reasons it would be redundant; her melody may be taken as her answer. It is repeated pianissimo on the brass, surely with no eye on a 'programme', but rather owing to the desire of a musician to repeat a melody he likes. In its elaborated form it has almost ceased to represent the youngest daughter. It is succeeded by the Lear theme (with its complement) on the unison strings interspersed by angry outbursts on the wind instruments and drums, the latter, by the way, with sponge-headed drumsticks. (The part, in which the nuances are very exactly indicated, requires careful handling. The passage can be nearly ruined by a too energetic drummer.) The Introduction to the overture might be instanced as an equipoise between 'musical and dramatic imagery'. Whether Berlioz would have agreed with my interpretation of it or not, some connexion can be traced between it and the opening scene of Shakespeare's drama. On the other hand, surely the music possesses sufficient interest in itself to be enjoyed apart from any programme.

The whole of the subsequent Allegro is, I am inclined to believe, devoted to a portrayal of Lear. As far as I am aware the only clue that Berlioz himself gave us was in a letter to Liszt, in which he said that he intended to express a 'deranged mind' by a passage towards the end of the overture. As this is a transformation of one of the subsidiary subjects, obviously they have nothing to do with Cordelia, as suggested by some commentators, or at any rate one of them has no connexion. Probably both the melodies illustrate the 'poor old man, as full of grief as age'. The Lear theme of the introduction is made use of throughout the Allegro. Once we have it complete, and two fragments of it are often employed in transformed but quite recognizable shape. The theme commences:

Ex. 4.

Andante (♩=63).

and immediately after the conclusion of the first subject we find the five initial notes of it thus:

Ex. 5.

Allegro (♩=168).

This serves as the germ of the transitional passage, great play being made with the triplets that are a feature of the Lear theme. The other transformation is more subtle, but none the less apparent. The last two bars of the complementary half of the theme are:

Ex. 6.

Andante.

In the development section there are repetitions of the emphatic seven notes that begin the first subject separated by phrases formed on this pattern

Ex. 7.

Allegro.

clearly derived from our preceding example. Lest we should miss the connexion between the two, Berlioz at the end of the introduction repeats the last two

bars of the theme in order to impress them on the
listener's memory. Indeed, as the Lear theme is of
such importance, its repetitions in the introduction may
be ascribed to the same reason, without dragging in
Goneril and Regan. In any case, this careful, almost
meticulous, use of his material is absurdly incompa-
tible with the idea of a composer whose 'eloquence
pours forth in a turbid, impetuous torrent which levels
all obstacles and overpowers all restraint'.

I have dwelt on this overture for several reasons.
In the first place, it was composed at a time which
Berlioz described as the happiest of his life, during
the weeks he spent at Nice recovering from his quinsy
and his jilting by Camille. He had nothing to do
except regain his health, mental and physical, and
compose, free from worry. The work illustrates his
methods in many ways—his plan of choosing some
tale to serve as a catalyst for his musical ideas ; and
then, as he proceeds to translate the tale into his own
language, paying more heed to the smoothness of the
translation than to its fidelity, his system of development, which often passes unperceived because it is not
confined to a particular section of the movement ; and
his retention of a free development of the sonata
form.

What we call inspiration must have something
tangible to work on. The sculptor does not sit down
before a block of marble trusting to inspiration to
guide his chisel. He must have some notion of what
his completed work will represent. He may modify
his idea to some extent during his labours, and at the
end elect to call his figure by some other name. But
these are minor matters. To commence with, his imagination must be aiming at some definite mark. So with
a musician. He may jot down in his note-book some
theme that may have struck him like a bolt from the
blue. Nevertheless, it can hardly be said to exist until he has anchored it to earth, until he has decided

what to do with it. How or when a theme musically depicting Lear or any other character occurred to Berlioz, we do not know. But, having found it, he would cast around for some form to fit it, 'that form without which music does not exist'. With his classical leaning he would be inclined to choose some classical form, but, claiming liberty, would feel free to modify it to suit his requirements. Although a contemporary of Haydn's for six years of his life, his ideas and emotions differed from those of the older composer as widely as the poles. Why should he therefore slavishly copy the same form to express them? The form he chose did not, however, invariably satisfy even himself. He 'burnt' the overtures to *Rob Roy* and *The Tower of Nice*, utilizing two themes of the former in the *Harold in Italy* Symphony and transforming the latter into the overture to *The Corsair*, which, as I have pointed out elsewhere,[1] has in reality no 'programme' attached to it.

As an example of the 'literary element' in Berlioz's music which it is necessary to understand before we can appreciate the full flavour of the music itself, a footnote to *The King of Thule* in the *Eight Scenes from Faust* is cited by some critics. It is to the effect that the singer should sing the ballad *without expression*, since Marguerite is supposed to be merely humming idly, as she makes her preparations for the night, without paying any heed to the meaning of the words. It was a silly direction, as Berlioz was the first to perceive, and is contradicted by the music. The sigh at the end is meaningless, if the girl were unconscious of what she was singing; and the same reason applies to the pauses on some of the notes. A few months after the *Eight Scenes* were published semi-privately—they never entered into general circulation—Berlioz did his best to destroy every copy. When he introduced the song in *The Damnation of Faust* he made several

[1] *Berlioz—Four Works*, London, 1929.

alterations. He commenced his melody on the second half of the bar, instead of the first, swayed by a keener sense of rhythm: he cut out the part of a clarinet that played in unison with the *tutti* violas: and, with a few other changes, discarded the ill-advised footnote which, if it did no other harm, was calculated to engender an insufferable monotony. In the *Eight Scenes* the ballad stands by itself; in the later work it is intimately connected with the preceding recitative. Marguerite finds in the fidelity of the old king that which she is determined to practise as regards Faust. The singer, if she would truly carry out Berlioz's intentions, if she would complete her picture of the girl still troubled by her dream, must put her soul into the song. It is an odd proceeding, taking a direction from one work and—against the wishes of the composer—transplanting it in another score, and then arguing that he did this or that on the strength of an indication he had consigned to the waste-paper basket. If one must delve into that useful article before its contents are conveyed to the dust-bin, why not retrieve the eliminated clarinet part ? Berlioz, I repeat, being an educated man, without being in any way an erudite one, could not avoid betraying the fact in his works. No artist can! The message from the shrine may be the same, but an educated man will deliver it in different fashion from one who had received little mental training. The difference may at times be subtle, and only apparent to *hommes intelligents*, but nevertheless it exists. I have suggested that Berlioz did certain things because he was an artist besides being a musician. But it is often possible to account for his attitude by reason of his having received some scientific (and therefore logical) training as a medical student. Having settled on his plan, he would proceed to execute it as a musician.

It is unfortunate that Berlioz was almost forced to affix a programme to his Fantastic Symphony. Forced,

since, although the programme may have intended
partly to induce an unmusical public to take an interest
in his work, it was required in order to explain the connexion between the last two movements and the first
three. No audience could be expected to understand
why a March to Execution[1] should follow a Scene in
the Country, though it may not be more difficult to
grasp than why a hero, having been decently buried,
should then go a-hunting. The objection to the programme is that both critics and audience took it to
have been written first, and the music afterwards,
whereas the contrary was the truth. Owing to this
erroneous belief, which Berlioz may have encouraged
to some extent, he has been deemed an uncompromis-
ing champion of programmes, and certain superficial
critics have even gone so far as to declare that he was
unable to compose without one. The reason of a
musician's inspiration can seldom be explained, even
by himself. A strong emotion will often serve as a
catalyst for the musical reaction; and, as Berlioz was
affected by poetry, especially dramatic poetry, almost
as powerfully as he was by music, he would naturally
be apt to be inspired by the former. A physical shock
may serve, as when the fact of falling into the Tiber
enabled him to find a melody which had eluded him
for a couple of years. At the time, scenery did not
inspire him. As he wrote to Wagner,[2] when the
latter was in Switzerland engaged on the composition
of *The Ring*:

'It must be wonderful to be able to write in the presence of
grand scenery ! . . . Alas ! such a joy is denied me ! Beautiful
country, towering peaks, a turbulent sea absorb me completely,

[1] It is astonishing that the B.B.C., which is inclined to plume itself on
the purity of its English, should persist in translating *Marche au Supplice*
as ' The March to the Gallows '. *Supplice* may mean any form of judicial
punishment. But the hero of the symphony had his head cut off. He was
not hanged. I doubt whether the boldest of the B.B.C.'s announcers would
refer to Charles I as dying on the gallows.

[2] *Correspondance inédite*, letter of 10 Sept. 1855.

instead of exciting me to thought. I feel but cannot express myself. I am only able to paint the moon when seeing its image at the bottom of a well.'

That is, since he was undoubtedly able to depict the varying aspects of Nature, he relied on remembered impressions. It is significant that the symphony of which he dreamt for two nights in succession and did not dare to put to paper lest he should be tempted to perform it, and so entail expenses he was unable to afford, was inspired by no programme. It would be absurd to imagine that this was not often the case. Themes occurred to him just as they do to every musician.

Berlioz's 'form' was dictated principally by the musical content, and in most cases it was, as Mr. Bernard Shaw said apropos of the work of another composer,[1] 'very successful in point of form (in the real as distinguished from the common, academic sense of the term)'. At times Berlioz may have been swayed by some story, and, as the same critic remarked,[2] 'it is impossible to tell a story in sonata form, because the end of a story is not a recapitulation of the beginning ; and the end of a movement in sonata form is '. As Haydn and other composers have admitted to having had at the back of their minds some tale, even when writing 'pure' music, this inability to tell a story in sonata form may possibly account for some of the so-called 'developments' of the strict form. Obviously, if a movement is in *perfect* (academic) form, with Exposition, Development, and Recapitulation, the addition of a coda (a tail) is as much out of place as would be one attached to a woman who satisfied all the canons of beauty. There is no escape from this argument. If a movement requires a coda to complete it, what has gone before is incomplete, as imperfect as the Venus of Milo. Berlioz, with his keen sense of logic and constant

[1] *Music in London, 1890–1894*, vol. ii.
[2] Op. cit.

desire to free music from the trammels of tradition, must have realized something of this, and hence in some of his movements it is difficult to state positively where the coda (if there is one) commences. For convenience of analysis it may be advisable, when dealing with his instrumental works, to retain the terminology of the sonata form—especially as there is not much doubt that that particular form was present in his subconsciousness—but to appreciate the beauty of his form we must regard his movements as a whole, and not as a series of sections welded together.

'Programme music' is difficult to define. It ranges from a musical imitation of tl sounds of nature or humanity to the impressions aroused by some incident, tale, or scene. Few composers have avoided the former, more particularly in vocal music, but perhaps it is legitimate only when it is used as a means to an end, merely as a method of augmenting the effect of some emotion or dramatic situation. The babble of the brook in the Pastoral Symphony is something more than the perpetual murmur of a stream. It typifies the composer's tranquillity of mind. As Johannes Weber pointed out,[1] if we take the rhythm of the Ride to the Abyss simply as an imitation of galloping horses, the idea may be considered almost puerile. If, however, we regard the whole piece as illustrative of Faust's agony of mind and increasing horror, the constant beating of the horses' hoofs intensifies the effect. It might be added that the subtle changes in the rhythm, together with the passing of the women at prayer, the hideous shape and the foul birds, all help to impart a strong sense of *motion* to the Ride, absent from a more celebrated one, based on a figure of two octave skips, more suggestive of a see-saw or rocking-horse than a flight through the air. The fall of the axe at the end of the March to Execution is certainly a touch of realism, but it is no more unmusical than the crashing

[1] *Les Illusions musicales*, Paris, 1883.

chord in the *Oberon* Overture, and, cutting across the
the *idée fixe*, its meaning would be clear even if there
were no programme to the symphony and we had
nothing beyond the bare titles of the movements,
which Berlioz suggested in one of its versions were
all that was necessary when the work was played
without its continuation *Lélio*. In *Harold in Italy* the
sound of the chapel bell and the phrases of the Pilgrims'
March interrupted by the mutterings of an *Ave* or
Paternoster are realistic effects, but are no more so than
those discovered by some commentators in Bach and
other composers. In symphonic music *musical* imitations of the sounds of nature or humanity are at any
rate harmless; they only become at times unnecessary
in operatic music, because we see the real thing. There
was no need for Meyerbeer to imitate on the orchestra
the sharpening of the scythe in *Dinorah*; we see and
hear the actual operation being performed.

The idea of Berlioz being an ardent supporter of
programme music, in so far as telling a tale in music
is concerned, rests almost entirely on the programme
he wrote to the Fantastic Symphony. Generally his
instrumental movements are but remembered impressions of some scene or story. Even where he gives
the programme, as in the Fantastic Symphony and
in the *Romeo and Juliet* (in a choral prologue), it is
usually impossible to pin the music down to a particular interpretation. In the Ball Scene of the latter
symphony what is the programme? Berlioz takes two
melodies from his prize-winning cantata *The Death of
Sardanapalus*, one a love-song and the other suggesting
a dance. He heads his scene with a slow movement
which we are told represents 'Romeo alone—Sadness'.
It includes the love-song on the oboe. Then follows
the Ball, and, after the main theme has been given
twice, we hear it combined with the love-song. There
is as little of a 'programme' here as there is in the
combination of the *Harold* theme with the Pilgrims'

H

March. Then there is a short *fugato* (derived from the dance theme) with a descending phrase of four bars as a counter-subject. The latter becomes more and more persistent and serves eventually as a *basso ostinato* (a constantly recurring bass) beneath rushing ascending triplets on the violins. Shortly before the end of the movement the love-song is again heard on the oboe, accompanied by the rhythm of the dance on the drums and the counter-subject on the lower strings. The latter *may* have some dramatic significance, though nobody seems to have discovered it. More probably it has no significance beyond a musical one. Berlioz erected a structure on a *basso ostinato* precisely as other composers have done, from Bach to Brahms.

Chapter Five

ORCHESTRATION

IN April 1781 Mozart, writing to his father, expressed his delight at having heard one of his symphonies given by forty violins, doubled wind, eight bassoons, and so on. It would not be difficult to find instances of a similar attitude amongst the majority of composers who have been skilled in orchestration. Incidentally, it may be observed that those who imagine that Mozart's works ought to be performed under 'Mozartean' conditions may not be affording his shade any peculiar gratification. That Berlioz should dream of more gigantic orchestras than his predecessors was due to several reasons. Without doubt he possessed grandiose ideas. But, apart from that, we must allow for the curiosity of a born orchestrator. Such a one, having been impressed by the majesty of (say) three trombones, would wonder how a dozen would sound, and seize an opportunity for testing the effect. However original a man may be, he must be affected to some extent by the spirit of his time, and in France during the first Republic and first Empire works given by a large body of performers were not uncommon. Berlioz must have often heard from his old master of the two orchestras of Gossec, the three of Méhul, and the four of Lesueur himself. Indeed, the last-named appears to have contemplated some composition planned to celebrate a Napoleonic victory, which, in addition to a choir, organ, and orchestra inside Notre Dame, included a chorus, military bands, church bells, and cannon outside. And, wherever the idea of an orchestra on an operatic stage may have originated, it became a feature of the Grand Opéra at Paris, as Wagner realized, when he wrote his *Rienzi*, with its orchestra of thirty-four on the stage. In 1841 the King of the French gave what might be

called a garden-party in the Galéries du Louvre, when
the guests were entertained by an orchestra of 260 and
a chorus of 140. The latter numbered less than that
demanded by Berlioz for his *Requiem* (210 voices), but
his orchestra (193 in the first edition of the score and
204 in the later ones) seems modest compared with
that of the garden-party. As a matter of fact, the actual
number of performers for the first performance of
the *Requiem* was only 300—the same number as
was employed for Mozart's on 15 December 1840
—which, as Bottée de Toulmon said in his notice
of the first performance of Berlioz's work,[1] was considered by many as being too few for the vast church
of the Invalides, It is unfortunate that Berlioz gave in
his Treatise an example of his four orchestras of brass
instruments and his array of drums. The book was
read by every musician, with the result that the French
composer was credited with requiring abnormal means
for the expression of his ideas, and we had comparisons
between his 'acres of drums and yards of brass' and the
instruments used in Beethoven's Fourth Symphony.
The gibe falls flat when addressed to those who know
Berlioz's scores, for few composers have produced such
fine effects with restricted means. It is true that he said
to Schumann[2] that he 'needed large means to produce
any effect', but this is contradicted by numerous movements and passages in his works. And, as he was commencing to write his *Requiem*, he would be anxious to
forestall any criticism of the means he intended to employ therein. (Detached remarks from the writings and
letters of a man have little force unless we know under
what circumstances they were penned.) That he was fond
of large orchestras cannot be denied, nor can the reasons
he adduced for preferring them be disputed. He insisted that it was only possible to obtain a perfectly true
note if there were a large body of executants. A string

[1] *La Gazette musicale*, 10 Dec. 1837.
[2] *Correspondance inédite*, letter of 19 Feb. 1837.

quartet, for instance, with each part doubled or trebled, even in the hands of first-class performers, would not sound well. The resultant notes, owing to infinitesimal differences in the intonation of the several players, would not be perfectly in tune. In the case of a large number of performers these differences would cancel one another. And so with singers. He also insisted that it was only possible to obtain a true pianissimo of the strings when the orchestra was a large one. To illustrate his ideas, however, he was led to extravagances, and included in the programmes of some of his monster concerts items that were totally unsuitable for a large orchestra and chorus ; and this, after admitting that such pieces as the scherzo of Beethoven's C minor Symphony and his own March to Execution lost much of their effect, when given by an orchestra above a certain number. His ideas on the size and disposition of orchestras are naturally of interest, but do not immediately concern us, save those recorded in his scores. By way of curiosity I would, however, mention an experiment he made at one of his ordinary concerts, that on 4 May 1844, for which he himself wrote the notice, duly signed, in *La Gazette musicale*. It commences : ' I cannot endure that man ! He possesses the most irascible disposition, the most ungracious character, the most absurd imagination that one could meet in this world of ours sparsely peopled by admirable dispositions, charming characters, and cheerful imaginations.' A specimen of Berlioz's curious humour ! The orchestra—' that unhappy orchestra which M. Berlioz torments, racks, cajoles, bullies, and rends¹ in so many deplorable ways!'—was composed of 4 flutes, 4 oboes, 4 clarinets, 4 bassoons, 4 horns, 4 (natural) trumpets, 4 trombones, 2 cornets, 2 harps, 1 ophicleide, and 4 players for the percussion instruments, against seventy strings. Unfortunately we are not told whether the

---

¹ A rough rendering of *brise, tord, souffle, gonfle et crève*, impossible to translate literally.

composer was satisfied with the effect in the overture
to *Les Francs Juges* and the *Harold in Italy* Symphony,
the two principal orchestral items. I do not know
whether he repeated the experiment. In any case it
would be unwise to follow his example. His balance
is so nicely calculated, that none but himself is entitled
to disturb it seriously.

Out of all Berlioz's compositions, the *Requiem* alone
really requires a huge orchestra and chorus in order
to produce its proper effect, though Berlioz on occasion
gave portions in Germany with much reduced means.
From the commentary to the work in the German
edition we learn that his original indications for the
'Tuba mirum' were wildly extravagant—twenty-four
horns and thirty-two kettle-drums figured amongst
them![1] His *Te Deum*, though undoubtedly requiring
the forces he has marked when performed in a large
building, can be given with all due effect in an ordinary
concert-room with an orchestra of fairly moderate dimensions. Indeed, from the indications in the French
edition of the score as regards the trombones, I am
inclined to think that he did not intend much more
than an ordinary orchestra when he commenced his
score, deciding on a larger one only when sketching
the wonderful 'Judex crederis'.[2] The large orchestra of
the Funeral and Triumphal Symphony may be said to
have been almost a matter of chance. He was commis-
sioned to write a work for a military band, and those
of four or five regiments were put at his disposal. For
the first performance—that is, before the *ad libitum*
string parts were written—there were 207 musicians,

---

[1] Gossec, for his second *Te Deum*, demanded *fifty* serpents and an army
of snare-drums.

[2] Six trombones are employed only in the first, second, and sixth numbers
of the *Te Deum* proper, but while they are duly marked at the head of the
first two, the indications in the course of them merely refer to *three*
instruments—'Les 3 unis', 2e et 3e unis' (only two trombones), and so on.
In the sixth number, the 'Judex', we find ' 1ers Tromb.', i.e. two instruments for the part.

a hundred less than the military band Berlioz heard at
Berlin, when the overture to *Les Francs Juges* was given,
arranged by Wieprecht. The fourth example of 'architectural' music is *L'Impériale*, a cantata written for
the ceremony of the distribution of prizes at the Paris
Exhibition of 1855. In the score there are directions
for the performance of the work by an ordinary
orchestra, with the two choruses reduced to one with a
solo quartet. The cantata is not likely to be revived,
although it contains an effect at the end which Berlioz
counted amongst his best. As he facetiously wrote to
Liszt, 'I assure you that it is a Polka which makes
you want to dance.' Yet the means employed are of
the simplest, apart from the large forces used at the
first performance. The choruses (in unison) doubled
by the trombones declaim the main theme—one taken
from his cantata *The Death of Sardanapalus*—accompanied by repeated chords on the wood-wind and
high tremolos for the strings, while the snare- and
kettle-drums *battent aux champs*,[1] 'as if for the arrival
of the Emperor'. It is an excellent example of the
broad effects that are advisable when writing for a large
number of performers. It is an irony of fate that we
are seldom allowed to appreciate them at their proper
value, since, as was complained with respect to the
Requiem, they are almost invariably given in too large
a building.

Berlioz's orchestration depends on much more than
an inexhaustible fertility as regards tone-colour and in
the invention of either absolutely novel combinations
or the happy re-adjusting of those of his predecessors.
His mastery of the orchestra is largely due to his
intuitive feeling for balance and keen appreciation of
the effect of contrast. In many cases his explosions seem
tripled in force because of his previous carefully calculated reticence. Thus, some of the effect of the

---

[1] *Battre aux champs* is an expression applied to a somewhat irregular
'battery' for the drums of a regiment as a salute for a superior officer.

March to Execution and the Witches' Sabbath is owing to the silence of the trombones and tubas during the first three movements. The end of the Ride to the Abyss is far from a lullaby, but he holds in reserve his trumpets and cornets for the Pandæmonium, besides the full power of the trombones and tubas, which have only been used in the Ride for a dozen bars, more for their colour than their force. In the *Requiem* itself his army of instruments is employed at full strength in two numbers only, and if we take the total number of bars in the work we shall find that the softer nuances predominate, a striking contrast to *Rienzi*, produced five years later (in 1842).

Another characteristic of Berlioz's scores is delicacy, which may be found even in his most strenuous passages. He is like some builder of a vast cathedral, who takes an artistic delight in carving dainty figures or tracery which are revealed only to close scrutiny. For instance, not only are the four orchestras of brass instruments of the *Requiem* of different disposition, but while the others are marked *ff* the third orchestra is merely *f* for the fanfare of the 'Tuba mirum'. We can discover similar subtleties elsewhere, and we must not forget that they are all calculated, and often have some bearing on the laying-out of his harmony. On this and similar points the opinion of MM. Pierné and Woollett[1] is of value:

'With Berlioz, it must be insisted, there is nothing unnecessary, everything is in its place, the apparently most insignificant details have their concealed purpose, which is only unveiled by performance. With the greatest masters (even occasionally with Beethoven himself) there are passages where the interpretation demands all the attention of the conductor, all his energy, all

[1] Histoire de l'orchestration' in the *Encyclopédie de la musique*, Part II. Unfortunately the authors have disfigured an otherwise admirable section by relying too much on the German editions and those in miniature score, with the result that they have been guilty of statements directly contrary to facts, such as declaring that Berlioz used mutes for his horns 'fairly frequently'.

his will, to give its proper value to this or that figure, either lacking in clarity or too much obscured. He has to ask one executant to moderate his sonority, another to exaggerate it, and even then it is not always possible to balance the orchestra. With Berlioz, all that labour is already done. He wrote nothing that he has not weighed with exactness, of which he has not calculated the absolute intensity, nothing (there differing from Wagner) that cannot be performed perfectly and easily.'

Gabriel Pierné, of course, writes from practical experience. After having been for six or seven years assistant conductor to Édouard Colonne (who did so much for Berlioz's works), he became, in 1910, sole conductor of the Colonne orchestra.

According to the above extract it should not be difficult to give a perfect performance of Berlioz's scores, given, of course, a sympathetic conductor. But like every other composer skilled as an orchestrator, Berlioz is dependent on an orchestra of the strength and disposition indicated in his scores. It is obvious that a balance calculated on there being sixty strings is upset when less than half that number are available, and that passages for the wood-wind need some re-adjustment, if there are only two bassoons instead of the three or four demanded by the composer. It is true that an orchestra may vary between fairly wide limits without the balance being seriously disarranged, and of course the power (and delicacy) of a body of strings hangs on other factors besides mere numbers. But nevertheless there is a limit, and when it is over-stepped, the conductor is compelled to exercise 'all his energy, all his will' in order to obtain some semblance of the composer's intentions. It is possible that the fluctuations in the size of orchestras, and the frequent presentation of works with inadequate means, have something to do with the undoubted fact that orchestral colouring is not held in the same esteem as that derived from harmony. It may require a different order of mind to excel in the latter, but it is not of

necessity a higher one. Orchestration is too often
regarded as something plastered on to that which is
music, instead of being, as Rimsky-Korsakov described
it, 'one of the aspects of the *very soul of the music*'. We
read, even in musical journals, of composers who have
finished their opera, and are now engaged on the
orchestration of it. The miserable question of bread-
and-butter has much to do with it, but it is odd to
find composers, who have presumably expended much
thought on the exact balance and precise coloration
of their combinations, consenting to the performance
of their work with meagre means and with parts either
omitted or played on other instruments. They would
be unlikely to agree to a similar treatment of (say) an
eight-part chorus, even though a cynic might suggest that some of the notes of ultra-modern harmonies
might be profitably omitted. For purposes of tuition
it may be advisable to treat harmony, counterpoint,
orchestration, form, and so on, as separate things; but
for all that they are not detachable garments that clothe
some mysterious entity called music. They are music
itself, and, in judging the musicality of a work, we must
consider them as one and indivisible; they resemble
a chemical compound rather than a mechanical mixture,
even though the formula may vary with every composer.

Part of the want of proper appreciation of orchestration is due to its being confused with 'instrumentation'. The latter is concerned with the study of the
separate instruments, their capabilities, their compass,
their different registers, and so on; without this knowledge perfect orchestration is impossible. But because
a piece of music is admirably written as regards the
separate parts, it does not follow that it is well orches-
trated any more than a knowledge of the text-book
rules of harmony ensures a piece being well harmonized.
Strictly speaking, instrumentation should be confined
to the arranging a piece for a number of instruments,
such as one written for piano, or adapting an orchestral

piece to the restricted resources of a seaside band of twenty or thirty. Orchestration is the art of writing for an orchestra without reference to anything else. The first might be compared to the arranging oı an orchestral piece for piano, which, even if it be by Liszt himself, is never the same as a composition conceived for a piano. Half a dozen men can adequately instrumentate a piece, but only one can orchestrate it. Berlioz instrumentated Weber's *Invitation to the Waltz* without, as he boasted, altering a note. It is astonishingly clever. But it is after all only a translation. Weber alone could make the original, just as no one else could write the melodies or harmonies, the other aspects of the very soul of the music.

Orchestration, in its true sense, is a recent ingredient of music. To say that Berlioz invented it would be ridiculous, but he may be considered to have been the first composer who was *invariably* purely orchestral in his treatment of the orchestra, if only for the reason that he could not play the piano. He had, too, a great advantage over his predecessors in that at the commencement of last century there was a great advance in the manufacture of musical instruments and an improvement in the players' technique, poor as the latter may have been compared with that of the present day. The invention of the Touıte bow during the closing years of the previous century alone accounted for much. The French master availed himself of these new developments, and thus was able to indulge in subtleties beyond the powers of the orchestras of those before him.

In reading Berlioz's scores there are some points that must be borne in mind. In the first place, except for a few numbers in his two last operas and (as far as I am aware) on three previous occasions,[1] he always wrote for the now obsolete natural horn. There was

---

[1] For his song *On the Lagoons*, for his arrangement of Schubert's *Erl-King*, and for the fourth horn in the Hunt in *The Damnation of Faust*.

nothing peculiar in his attitude, for, except sporadically, as in *La Juive* in 1835, valve horns were not employed in France until the nineteenth century was past its meridian. Anticipating the performance of his works in Germany, where the new instrument was adopted much earlier, he was, however, careful to add occasional directions in case valve horns were employed. These concerned notes that he wished to be produced, not by means of the valves, but by the lips with the aid of the hand in the bell of the instrument. In the French editions these notes are marked *bouché* (stopped or closed). In the German edition, and in the score of the Fantastic Symphony in the miniature edition, the direction has been altered to *con sordino* (with the mute), an analogous but not identical effect. It is true that most modern horn-players have lost much of the art of producing the closed notes, but that does not excuse the alteration. Berlioz, having marked muted horns in his *Eight Scenes from Faust*, never repeated the direction, and does not even mention mutes for horns in his Treatise. A more serious alteration made by the editors of the German edition is an occasional change of key in the horn parts. Every possessor of a few miniature scores of the classical masters knows that in the parts for the (natural) horns there are blanks, easily explained by the fact that an 'open' note (i.e. a note of the harmonic scale, produced without the aid of the hand) is not available, and a 'closed' one is inadvisable. To throw the part into another key alters the part to one for a valve horn, when the blanks become meaningless. The part is changed into one that could be written only by a composer who understood neither the old nor the modern instrument. The transposition is exasperating in the scores of one so careful of details as Berlioz, and is a waste of labour, since a modern player, armed with his valve horn, will probably transpose *all* the parts, save those in F, to suit himself.

In all his larger works (apart from his 'architectural' ones) Berlioz required four bassoons, and, judging from the indications in his scores, did not look upon the two extra instruments as being *ripieni*, but as integral parts of the instrumentation. We can find many passages where a single bassoon is marked, but, on the other hand, it is not uncommon to have a solo oboe or clarinet doubled in the octave below by *two* bassoons, when Mozart or Beethoven would use but one. In Berlioz's day it was the custom, as it is now, for all well-equipped French orchestras to possess four bassoons, and hence his ideas on the employment of the instruments differed from those of German practice. He was so exact in all his other indications that I cannot believe that he was careless as regards those relating to the bassoons. Observe the directions to the bassoons in Juliet's funeral procession—now one, now two, now four—and it is impossible to believe that in numerous pages he left the quantum of bassoon tone entirely to the discretion (or the want of it) of the conductor. Other examples equally emphatic might be adduced. The suggestions[1] of the editors in the German edition as to the number of bassoons to be employed may be dismissed, for the very good reason that in so many cases they deliberately ignore Berlioz's wishes. In works, such as *The Roman Carnival* and *The Corsair* Overtures, where he asked for four bassoons, only two are marked, for the puerile reason that the instruments are in only two parts throughout; and in many passages, where the composer has indicated his requirements with perfect clarity, his indications have been altered. Thus, in the *Harold in Italy* Symphony (*Min. Sc.*, p. 55) where he wants the four bassoons to play in unison or octave with the solo viola, instead of marking his customary *unis*, he writes in full 'Les 4

---

[1] These are supposed to be always placed within brackets, but the plan is very far from being strictly carried out. Often it is impossible to know what emanates from the composer.

B^{ns} unis', in order to avoid the slightest possibility of a mistake. He foresaw what conductors might be tempted to do, and the editors of the German edition have justified his forebodings by placing against the part 'a 2' instead of 'a 4' without a hint to a conscientious conductor of what were the express wishes of the composer. (Berlioz, by the way, indicated very rarely 'a 2', with its ambiguous double meaning.) He may have left something to conductors versed in the traditions of French orchestras as regards bassoons, but I do not fancy he felt himself in any way bound by those traditions. We shall not err greatly in taking his indications against the bassoon parts at their face value. That is, when there are two parts, each is taken by two instruments; a single part with *unis* above is played by all four bassoons; a single part, with rests beneath, is executed by two. And this irrespective of nuance. To ears trained on German practice the amount of bassoon tone may seem at times too much, but it was not only in the matter of bassoons that Berlioz differed from Teutonic methods. In any case the ideas of the late M. Charles Malherbe, who, as we shall see, was mainly responsible for the German edition, may be discarded. With few exceptions his simple plan of four bassoons for loud passages and two for soft ones is carried out with maddening monotony.

For the benefit of admirers of the scherzo of the *Romeo and Juliet* Symphony I would add one more mildly technical detail. In modern practice harp harmonics are indicated by writing the notes to be plucked by the player, with a small 'o' or 'sons harmoniques' above them, the actual sounds being an octave higher. But for some years after the introduction of the effect into the orchestra by Boieldieu in *La Dame blanche* composers were uncertain about the best mode of notation, and Berlioz was no exception. In the Ballet of the Sylphs the *plucked* notes are given; in the scherzo, the *actual sounds* are noted in all the editions, with the possible exception of the original one published in 1848.[1] That is, the harpist must play his part an octave lower. *Of this there is not a shadow of doubt.* If the reader will collate the last bars of the second example in Berlioz's Treatise with the corresponding ones in the miniature score, he will see that in the latter the harp notes are written an octave higher. In the section devoted to the harp in the Treatise the author explains how he meant the harmonics of the second example to *sound*—an octave above those in the example, but in unison with those in the miniature score.

To detail all Berlioz's orchestral innovations would be a hopeless task. His genius exhibits itself not so much in the invention of novel combinations, as in his general treatment of the orchestra. To repeat a simile employed by other writers, he writes for the orchestra as Paganini did for the violin, and Chopin and Liszt for the piano. Neither of the last-named can compare with Beethoven as a composer, but both excelled him as regards adapting their ideas to the medium of the piano, as indeed many minor composers, such as Saint-Saëns and Raff, have done. It is true that we should judge a musical work principally from the point of view of its musicality, but nevertheless it is a debatable question how far a composer is entitled to ignore the limitations of the medium he chooses for the expression of his ideas. It may be argued that the musicality of a passage or movement depends on there being an exact equation between the idea and its expression, that is, that orchestral ideas expressed on the piano, or vice versa, are not truly musical. From such a test Berlioz would emerge triumphant, failing only in one particular, in that at times he was inclined

[1] Throughout the German edition the notes to be plucked are indicated by notes with open diamond-shaped heads. As Bizet had already used these to indicate the *real* sounds, and as such notes are employed in violin practice with another signification, the method has little to commend it.

to treat his voices as instruments—a fault which he shares with other musicians.

It is a mistaken idea to suppose that Wagner's orchestration is any particular advance on that of Berlioz, and that the latter in this respect was a sort of John the Baptist to the Bayreuth master. As Pierné and Woollett have said,[1] speaking of Wagner's two last works:

'The sonorous impasto is more and more supple, firm and warm (*onctueuse*), at times a trifle heavy, always rich and compact. Berlioz contributes more brilliancy, more originality, and also more delicacy; it is erroneous to believe that Wagner's orchestra constitutes a great improvement on Berlioz's. It is merely a different one, which has a power, a dramatic intensity, incontestable and unequalled. We must not forget that the apparent brutality of it should be tempered by an execution in accordance with the master's wishes; the orchestra below the level of the stage, and the brass hidden behind the proscenium.'

The two authorities, however, omit to add that, even under the conditions demanded by Wagner, the disposition of the orchestras of *The Ring* and *Parsifal* has been altered to some extent by successive conductors. An account of what really takes place in the cellar at Bayreuth would be of interest. The commanding genius of Wagner imposed itself on the composers of the latter end of the last century in the matter of orchestration as it did in other directions, but probably the influence of Berlioz has been more permanent. The Russian school from the first moulded their orchestral methods on Berlioz and Liszt, who himself owed much to the French master. Indeed, Wagner acknowledged his indebtedness to Berlioz, and said, 'I made a minute study of his [Berlioz's] instrumentation as early as 1840, and have often taken up his scores since.' It is doubtful, however, whether the latter part of his sentence is strictly accurate, since we find him in 1855 asking Liszt to lend him some of the French

[1] *Op. cit.*

composer's scores, in which Liszt could not oblige him, since he had already lent them. Wagner's closest acquaintance with Berlioz's works must have been at Dresden in 1842, when *avec zèle et de très-bon cœur* he assisted at the rehearsals for Berlioz's concerts. His help would have been the more valuable, since he had heard all the several items in Paris two years previously, and of course to a musician such as he it would be easy to learn much from mere audition. Having recovered from its attack of Wagneritis, 'the entire French school' —to quote again MM. Pierné and Woollett—'is the daughter of Berlioz', and though naturally the Germans have been prone to follow Wagner, 'Mahler and Strauss owe more to Berlioz, who remains the great inspirer of the orchestral art of to-day'. Composers have realized that the orchestra of *The Ring* is as much a special one as that of Berlioz's *Requiem*.

It is a great advantage to any composer for the orchestra to be a conductor. He is, or should be, able to couch his ideas in practical form, and to mark the nuances and other indications precisely as he, in the role of the composer, would have them. Without venturing to weigh the relative merits as conductors of Berlioz, Wagner, Strauss, and Mahler, I may point out that the first-named suffered from one disadvantage, which was shared by Wagner only during the early part of his career, and that was, as suggested above, the indifferent technique of orchestral players. Even within living memory matters have improved enormously in that particular. In 1895, when Sir August Manns gave the first performance of *Till Eulenspiegel* in England, he apologized to the audience for any possible shortcomings on the part of the players, since it was the most difficult piece that they had ever attempted. Yet a short time back that same piece was performed by the students of one of our musical academies. In Berlioz's case the limitations of his players were in one sense an advantage, since, bearing

those limitations constantly in mind, he was careful
not to give his musicians passages that were too difficult for them. In the commentary to the *Romeo and
Juliet* Symphony in the German edition we find the
first few bars of the original accompaniment for the
strings of the Invocation. The editors suggest that
the composer abandoned it, because he feared that his
orchestra would be unable to play the somewhat complicated rhythm correctly. Their surmise is probably
true. He did indeed write parts that must have seemed
to the players of his day almost impossible, but, thanks
to his intimate knowledge of the several instruments
and to his instructions at rehearsals, they would have
soon found the difficulties by no means insuperable.
Nowadays, of course, his music is easy to perform, and
that makes for excellence. Composers of the present
day are apt to forget that, because a passage can be
played by our highly skilled musicians, it does not at
all follow that it is advisable to write it. The player,
engrossed with the difficulties of his part, can hardly
be expected to endow it with all the requisite expression. Wagner was not so careful as Berlioz, and probably suffered on that account. It is difficult to believe
that had (say) the *Tannhäuser* Overture been performed
in 1845 as we hear it to-day, it would not have won
favour more quickly.

Berlioz differed from the other conductor-composers
I have named in the fact that he allowed years to
elapse before many of his scores were engraved, and
during the interval he had opportunities for testing
his indications from rehearsals and performances by
different orchestras under different conditions, and
making such further touches as he deemed advisable.
As a specimen of these touches take Faust's air in
The Damnation of Faust, which was first performed on
6 December 1846, whereas the full score was not published till 1854. Except for a few pizzicato notes, the
double-basses do not enter (*arco*) till four bars before

the voice part ceases. They are in unison with the violoncellos, which, together with the upper strings, are marked *pp*. Berlioz knew, however, either instinctively or from his experiences at rehearsals, that the double-basses would be inclined to enter too heavily, so, in order to be on the safe side, he placed *ppp* against their part. In the next bar all the strings are *pp* against the *p* of the wood-wind.[1] I have cited these two bars, since they are an example of what Pierné and Woollett have pointed out—that 'Berlioz wrote nothing that he has not weighed with exactness, of which he has not calculated the absolute intensity'. This extreme attention to minutiæ is evinced in other directions.

It has been remarked that composers who excel as conductors are inclined to be fond of the percussion instruments of the orchestra. The explanation is obvious. A conductor, who is worth his salt, must possess a keen sense of rhythm, though he may prostitute it at times to what he considers to be the proper 'reading' of a work, and, as a composer, he would wish to mark that rhythm. It is true that in the scores of Wagner the percussion instruments (apart from the timpani) are rarely employed, and then more for their colour than their rhythmic qualities, but his methods of composition were opposed to any strongly accentuated rhythm, and, although his ideas have largely affected the modern school of conductors and he himself often obtained excellent performances, as a conductor he was not in the same rank as Richter, Nikisch, von Bülow (in his saner moments), Toscanini, or Berlioz. The last named, as we know, inveighed against the use of

[1] Whilst admitting that these indications are to be found in Berlioz's autograph, the editors of the German edition have altered them, declaring that there is no reason for them. It may be so, though I doubt whether Berlioz often penned nuances without reason. He might at any rate be given the benefit of the doubt in a 'faithful' edition of his works. To assume that one is acting ' in conformity with the *evident intention* ' of one's author by deliberately ignoring what he has plainly set down would seem to be a dubious proceeding. (My italics.)

the bass drum by Rossini and his school. To a superficial reader of the French master's scores it might
seem that here we have a case of the pot calling the
kettle black. A closer examination of them will reveal
a great difference. Study the arrangement of the
Rakoczy march, and note the contradictory nuances
assigned to the brass from the end of the trombone
theme to that of the march. While the strings and
wood-wind are *ff* throughout, the brass are *p* or *f*, and
are never marked *ff*, though many notes are strongly
accentuated. (As Berlioz, with the extra valve-trombone
which enters at the commencement of the trombone
theme, had four of these instruments, besides an
ophicleide and tuba, he was probably anxious that they
should not be too blatant.) The percussion have also
contradictory nuances, and the bass drum and cymbals
are not invariably played at the same time.[1] Every
student of Berlioz's Treatise realizes that, though
written on a single line, the two instruments must be
taken by separate performers.

Berlioz did not originate contradictory nuances—
we find them here and there in Beethoven—but he
certainly was the first to employ them systematically,
and in this he has been followed in the sensitive orchestration of the present day. It is unnecessary to add
that in the French editions *some* of the contradictory
signs are clearly faults of the engraver, but a decision
must not be made too precipitately.

Rather than reeling off a list of some of Berlioz's
innumerable novelties in his treatment of the orchestra,
I have preferred to deal with questions that affect his
methods generally, as I wish to combat the popular
notion that his fame as an orchestrator rests mainly
on the invention of startling effects. As a matter of

[1] The point is doubtful, but, judging from the French edition, I fancy
that for the five bars commencing twenty-four bars from the end of the
march the bass drum plays alone, and not in unison with the cymbals, as
in the German edition. The notes have no tails pointing downwards to indicate the latter.

fact, it is exceedingly difficult in art to declare dog-
matically that this or that is absolutely new and original. Mr. S. C. Kaines Smith[1] tells us that 'Cubism,
unjustly fathered upon Cezanne, is as old as the
sixteenth century. . . . Futurism . . . was known in
principle to, and used in practice by, Leonardo da
Vinci.' M. Charles Kœchlin has pointed out that the
unprepared chord of the dominant 7th, the introduction of which is generally attributed to Monteverdi,
was written by Pierre de la Croix (Petrus de Cruce)
and Guillaume de Machaut in the thirteenth and four-
teenth centuries, and then forgotten for a couple of
hundred years. The chords and modulations in Berlioz's *Cleopatra*, which distressed Boieldieu, had been
used by Bach, Purcell, and Scarlatti, though so far as
Boieldieu and Berlioz were concerned they were absolutely novel. It is of interest to note the retouches to
the orchestration (and harmony) when the Invocation
of *Cleopatra*—the number in which these 'new' harmonies principally appeared—was introduced into *Lélio*,
when the latter was published twenty-six years later.
Berlioz's supremacy in the art of orchestration is due
in the first place to an intimate knowledge of instrumentation which aided his unerring sense of balance,
and secondly, to an instinctive feeling for a perfect
equation between a melody and the instrument that
interpreted it. Even when he undoubtedly employed
combinations found in the works of his predecessors,
he often made them his own. Divided violins had
figured in scores long before his time, but their use
at the commencement of the last movement of the
Fantastic Symphony and in the 'Sanctus' of the *Requiem* was novel. In his Treatise he tells us that Spontini was the first to discover the peculiar sympathy
between piccolos and cymbals, and in the overture
to *Les Francs Juges* he copies the effect. But in *The
Damnation of Faust*, for the entrance of Mephistopheles,

[1] *Art and Commonsense*, The Medici Society, 1932.

the addition of rapid chords for the trombone makes it his own. We have the chords when Mephistopheles warns Faust of Marguerite's approach, but as the piccolo is absent the cymbals are not marked, though the editors of the German edition have for some reason suggested their use.

Kastner tells us, in the Supplement to his Treatise on Instrumentation, that a trombonist of the Opéra named Schiltz pointed out to him the possibility of making use of the first harmonics of the trombone (commonly called 'pedals'), though, as he suggests, they were probably known before his time. On the ordinary scale of the tenor trombone the lowest note is E below the bass clef: the highest of the pedals is the B♭ below that, the other possible ones being the next three notes descending chromatically. (The interval between the E and the B♭, *with the exception of the B♮*, is nowadays bridged on the tenor-bass trombone by means of a valve manipulated by the thumb.) Hérold in *Zampa* (1831) wrote the highest pedal for ten bars, but it passes unperceived, since it is marked *pp* and serves as the bass of the horns and bassoons. When Berlioz used all four pedals in the 'Hostias' of his *Requiem* (1837) with only three flutes three and four octaves above them, the effect was considered as an absolutely new one, as indeed it was. Principally perhaps on account of this use of the pedals, which Berlioz ill-advisedly repeated in the last number of his work—probably because he was pressed for time— and gives in his Treatise, a modern writer has accused him of having 'a whole hive of pedal-bees in his bonnet'. As a matter of fact he employs them no more than seven or eight times, and usually for harmonic reasons. The only bass instrument of brass he could depend on obtaining in French orchestras during the greater part of his career was the ophicleide, with the lowest note B♮ below the bass clef. If he wanted a low B♭ or A, unless he marked the rarely used ophicleide in A♭, he could not obtain it except by names of the trombone pedals. For this reason we find pedals at the commencement of the *Te Deum*, and at the end of the *Hamlet* March and the prelude to *The Trojans at Carthage*. A modern composer wanting the harsh effect of the diminished 7th (A-G♭) in the bass (second bar after the double bars in the March to Execution) would possibly give the higher note to the trombone and the lower to a tuba, as was indeed done in the first impressions of the score of the March in the German edition, though I suspect that in this case it was done to oblige the third *German* trombonist of those days, who would often play a bass instrument on which it was impossible to obtain the B♭ and A—a curious method of editing the score of a French composer! Berlioz only marked the pedals twice on account of their tone quality, that is, for their dramatic effect—in the *Requiem* and in the 'Judex crederis' of the *Te Deum*. In the Ride to the Abyss, where they are in the midst of low notes for the bass clarinet, four bassoons and ophicleides, any peculiarity of tone is imperceptible. Had he had contrabass and bass trombones, contrabass and 'Wagner' tubas at his disposal, his picture of the 'hideous shape' pursuing Faust might have been drawn otherwise. The highest pedal may be said to have entered into general circulation, and the rest we can find here and there in Elgar, Rimsky-Korsakov, Schönberg, and others. In any case Berlioz's hive of pedal-bees was not a large one.

The above somewhat technical remarks illustrate some points as regards Berlioz's orchestration. One of the principal differences between the modern orchestra and that of Beethoven and Weber is that the former possesses a greater number of powerful bass instruments capable of descending into depths unknown to the classical masters. Berlioz was worse off than they since he had not at his disposal a true bass trombone.

(The *trombone basse* of French orchestras was merely
a tenor one playing the lowest notes.) He wrote for
three tenor trombones, and preferred them, as he tells
us in his Memoirs, finding that if the third were a
bass one, it was apt to overpower the other two. And
naturally he required the true tenor instrument, and
not modern tenor-bass trombones, which are bass ones
in F cut down to the length of the tenor. We all
realize the impossibility of performing the scores of
Bach or Handel as they were played under the composer's own direction, but few of us consider whether
we hear those of Weber and Berlioz as they heard
them, putting aside the greater skill of modern players
and the improved intonation of modern wood-wind
instruments. Weber's alto, tenor, and bass trombones
are now too often three tenor-bass ones, with the
thumb-piston attached to the third: the modern German horns are of larger bore, which, though it may
give them increased facility in coping with the elaborate parts of modern scores, entails some loss of
delicacy: the tone of the clarinet is less reedy and
more flute-like: the trumpets are no longer true ones,
but instruments of half their length, and (in Weber's
case) the tone of the bassoon is not the same, as the
reed is narrower. The differences may be slight—
possibly no greater than those which exist nowadays
between two performances of a modern work given in
(say) Munich and Paris—but they do exist. And in
criticizing or studying the scores of a hundred years
ago we must bear them in mind, not so much on
account of the difference in tone quality, but as regards
the laying out of the score. As the oboes and bassoons
of Berlioz were not the same as those of his German
contemporaries, his treatment of the instruments was
not the same. The fact that he wrote for three (true)
tenor trombones explains his preference for close harmony on the instruments, and accounts for some of
his unisons on the three instruments. Had his third

trombone been a bass one he might have disposed his parts differently, as he certainly would have done for that wonderful common chord of E♭ that ushers in the 'Tuba mirum', with fourteen of his sixteen trombones concentrated on E♭ in the bass clef.

Chapter Six

THE WORKS

IN dealing with the works of a musician it is always difficult to know upon which to concentrate. Should the writer be an admirer of the composer, he wishes naturally to dwell on those works which exhibit the highest qualities. On the other hand, as in most cases these are the best known, to discuss them at length savours of supererogation. As regards Berlioz, however, the writer has the dubious satisfaction of knowing that the major portion of his output is not sufficiently familiar to render an account of it superfluous. But one's difficulties are not lessened on that account. To arouse enthusiasm in the breast of a reader for any unknown work of art, even with copious examples or illustrations, is more than difficult. It verges on the impossible.

The approach to Berlioz is less easy than that to other composers of the nineteenth century, since his principal works cannot be studied at the piano. Wagner declared that his own operas would become popular through the medium of the keyboard instrument, and any one who remembers the early days of the Wagner cult will realize that there was a great deal of truth in the remark. Amateurs learnt more of (say) *Tristan and Isolda* from Hans von Bülow's arrangement than from actual performances. Nobody can realize the beauty of *The Trojans* from the vocal score. It is true that the composer's own arrangement is bad, but it is doubtful whether a better one would make much difference, for many of Berlioz's purely orchestral passages cannot be translated adequately into the language of the piano. In one of his letters to Liszt,[1] he objected to the latter's transcription of a passage for the violins in the *King Lear* Overture.

[1] *Au milieu du chemin*, p. 75.

Ex. 8.
(♩ = 168).

&c.

He complained: 'Whenever this figure appears you use octave triplets. Now, the triplet is quite insufficient to produce the effect of the quavers; ternary rhythm is there irreconcilable with the deranged mind (*caractère échevelé*) that I wish to illustrate.' The triplets also obscure the derivation of the figure from one of the second subjects of the work; but to play the part as written at the proper tempo (♩= 168) is excessively difficult on the piano. When composing or arranging for the instrument Berlioz was fully aware of his own shortcomings. As regards *Cellini*, he told Liszt in a letter of 1853[1] that he himself had undertaken the piano arrangement 'which I will afterwards submit to some pianist of my acquaintance that he may correct the gaucheries'. Nevertheless, he preferred to arrange some of his works, since he distrusted arrangers after his experience with *Les Francs Juges* Overture—see his letter to Hofmeister in the *Correspondance inédite*.

In spite, however, of Berlioz's pianistic clumsiness, I am inclined to think that we shall gain a better insight into the real Berlioz, if we approach him through his songs. By so doing we shall lose something of his wonderful variety, his excursions into fairyland, his colouring, and his illustrations of the grand, the grotesque, or the terrible. But, on the other hand, the variety that remains is great; we find facets of his genius differing from those in his orchestral works; and, after a study of the songs, it would seem impossible for any one to deny him the gift of melody, though it may not be always of conventional pattern, or to credit him with that 'eccentricity' attributed to him by his opponents for the past hundred years. It is to be

[1] *Briefe an Franz Liszt*, i, p. 262.

regretted that there is no English edition of his songs published at a reasonable price.

Volume xvii of the German edition of his works is devoted to songs for a single voice, of which the piano accompaniments are by the composer himself, with the exception of that to the final version of *The Captive*, which was originally reduced from the orchestral score by Stephen Heller. This has been replaced in the German edition by an arrangement by one of the editors, with the plea that Heller's 'had to be discarded, since it presents differences from the full score'. Possibly! none the less it was approved by Berlioz. In the volume there are twenty-nine melodies, of which three figure in larger works—the contralto solo, *Premiers transports*, from the prologue to the *Romeo and Juliet* Symphony, and from *Lélio* the *Song of Happiness* and *The Fisherman*. (The last named is described as the second version, but this is a slip of the editors. The second version of the song is in the published score of *Lélio* which appeared in 1855: that in vol. xvii was first published in 1833.) The volume also contains two versions of *The Song of the Bretons* composed originally for male chorus, and as such included in the previous volume, but finding a place here on the strength of a direction of Berlioz's to the effect that it may be sung by a solo voice taking the part of the first tenors. The fine, bold melody would be perhaps more effective transposed a third lower to C, and sung by a baritone. M. Tiersot tells us[1] that in the library of the Conservatoire there is a copy of the song for chorus and orchestra marked 'Orchestration copied by M. Weckerlin for the concerts of the Saint Cecilia Society', but whether the instrumentation is by Berlioz himself I do not know.

During his lifetime Berlioz brought out five collections of songs—or rather vocal pieces, since they included some due   id choruses—*Mélodies irlandaises*

[1] 'Berlioziana'.

(afterwards called *Irlande*), *Fleurs des Landes*, *Les Nuits d'été*, *Feuillets d'album*, and finally 32 (afterwards 33) *Mélodies*, which included most of the earlier numbers with the addition of *The Captive*, *The Fifth of May*, and some others. As it was more reasonable to separate songs for a single voice from choruses, these heterogeneous classifications have been wisely ignored in the German edition, and the songs have been arranged in chronological order, not always, it must be confessed, with complete success. It is often difficult, if not impossible, to fix the precise date of composition of many of the songs, and the editors at times give the date of publication, when that of composition may have probably been some years previously. The only one of the primitive collections that displays any homogeneity is *Summer Nights* (*Les Nuits d'été*), in which the words are all by Théophile Gautier, and all the songs treat of some phase of love. They require, however, two or three different voices for their adequate performance. These six melodies are amongst the finest that Berlioz ever wrote,[1] and, though they are considerably more effective in their orchestral dress, they are charming enough in their original form with piano accompaniment to win adherents to Berlioz, as the present writer can testify. The variety found in the several numbers is wonderful. What greater contrast could we have than that between No. 1, the *Villanelle*, joyous as the breath of spring, and No. 5, *At the Cemetery*, with the cold glitter of the moonlight so admirably expressed, not by any cunning orchestral device—there are only two flutes and two clarinets in the score in addition to the strings—but by the harmony and the rigid rhythm of the opening? Or take No. 3, *On the Lagoons*, with the recurring C♮, D♭, a sort of intermittent pedal on the dominant of the key of the piece (F minor), but persisting throughout the modulations to F major, A major, and A minor. The reiterated wail is in perfect keeping

[1] Novello has published an English edition of the collection.

with a *Lamento* (the sub-title of the song). From an harmonic point of view the proceeding was a bold one at the date of composition,[1] and is an example of Berlioz's foreshadowing of modern methods. There is another at the end of the song, which concludes with the common chord on the *dominant* of the key of the piece, suggesting a grief that refuses to be comforted. With a change of key to Bb, the middle portion rises to a passionate outburst that the composer seldom surpassed. No. 4, *Absence*, is certainly one of the songs of the world, despite the carpings of 'correct mediocrities' at the irregular resolution of the tritone in the third bar, to which I have already referred. Probably many, like Ernest Newman, will find in the opening phrase a suggestion of distance, as though the lover were calling to his mistress across some vast space. No. 2, *The Spectre of a Rose*, is the most elaborate of the collection, and for that reason may not make such an immediate appeal. It is a perfect setting of the beautiful words, from which the composer has 'sucked all the poetry'. And it is difficult to believe that any unbiased lover of music would fail to appreciate the delicate charm of No. 6, *The Unknown Land*.

The German edition gives two versions of *The Spectre of a Rose* and *At the Cemetery*, the latter having apparently caused the composer the greatest trouble in moulding the song to his satisfaction, judging by the variants of particular passages recorded in the commentary to the volume. Some of Berlioz's corrections were made after he had scored the melodies, and in so doing he reversed the ordinary procedure. Without being in any way dependent on the piano, many composers are tempted to 'try over' doubtful passages on the instrument. Berlioz, on the other hand, was only able to express himself freely when unhampered by the keyboard.

---

[1] The German edition gives it as 1834, but Tiersot in 'Berlioziana' declares that he can find no warranty for this date. The collection was first published in 1841.

The first three songs of vol. xvii are immature, and unlikely to be of much interest to any save students of Berlioz, with the exception of *Toi qui l'aimais*. This, in spite of its stiff accompaniment, possesses a real charm. As M. Tiersot has pointed out, we find in it an early illustration of Berlioz's practice of modulating from the major to the minor instead of the usually reverse process. The composer on the title-page announced himself as a 'pupil of M. Lesueur', which suggests that the song was published before August 1826, when he was admitted to the Conservatoire and was no longer a private pupil of Lesueur. The last two songs in the volume are settings of identical words—*Morning* and *Little Bird*, the latter being a joyous melody in F minor! Like *La Belle Voyageuse* and *The Young Breton Shepherd*, it has that strong affinity with folk-song which, as Schumann observed, is to be found in many of Berlioz's melodies. *Morning*, also commencing in the minor and only passing to the major at the end of each verse, is a more elaborate setting. There is a quaintness in the opening phrase, due principally to the major ninth resolving upwards, and the end of the song supplies a curious instance of tone-painting. To illustrate the warbling of the bird, above an arpeggio of the chord of the dominant the voice holds a high G (the 7th), while the piano trills, first on the B (the 9th) and then on the A (the root).

Amongst other songs in the volume must be noted *Les Champs* (The Fields or Country), an aubade. It is hard to understand how any one can deny its melodiousness or its joyousness, the latter being a characteristic to be found in many of the songs, and less rarely than in the choral or orchestral works. In these there are many pages that reflect gaiety, cheerfulness, happiness; but few exhibit the sheer joyousness of *The Fields*, *Little Bird*, *The Young Breton Shepherd*, and the *Villanelle*. Under what circumstances these songs were composed we do not know, but in the fitness of things

Berlioz should have been inspired by the tunes during one of his long tramps in the country, of which he was so fond. The melodies give us a glimpse of what he might have given us had his life been ordered differently. *The Danish Huntsman* is a rousing melody of a somewhat conventional type, suggesting little of the composer save in its instrumentation and the last couplet, in which the notes of the theme are given in augmentation, a device Berlioz uses at times to express something in the nature of a prayer. The orchestral balance is curious, with only eighteen strings (5–5–3–2–3) against the usual wood-wind (with four bassoons), *no* trumpets, four horns, three trombones, and drums.[1] *Zaïde* is a bolero and is one of Berlioz's few attempts at 'local colour', the others being the Siciliana in *Beatrice and Benedick* and the dance of the Nubian slaves in *The Trojans*, to which we might add the *Rustic Serenade to the Madonna* amongst the three pieces for harmonium, and the first theme of the Serenade in the *Harold in Italy* Symphony. In the *Rob Roy* Overture he introduces *Scots wha hae*, but there is nothing Scottish in the treatment of the tune. Some have found an Italian atmosphere in portions of *Benvenuto Cellini* and elsewhere, but it is hardly local colour in the modern sense. In *Zaïde* Berlioz caught the Spanish spirit, and the melodiousness of the song is sufficient to make us wonder at its neglect. In vol. xvii there are two versions of it for piano, the orchestral score being in vol. xiv, where it was published for the first time. From a letter to Desmarest[2] dated from Vienna, 16 December 1845, we learn that Berlioz sold the German rights to Haslinger, who apparently

---

[1] The disposition of the orchestra is given in the commentary that heads vol. xv in the German edition. The number of strings is never marked in the scores themselves, save in the case of the four 'architectural' works, the editors professing to believe that conductors would be too frightened to perform the others, if they knew that at times Berlioz demanded at least sixty strings!

[2] Given in *La Revue musicale*, 15 Aug. 1903.

never exercised them. The former begged Desmarest
to offer the French ones to Bernard Latte, who refused
them. To prevent their being lost, a hastily engraved
edition was published by Berlioz himself, a pitiable
necessity for a master at the zenith of his powers!
Two hundred francs was all he asked for the song, his
usual price for his Romances.

The Captive and the *Elegy* stand apart from the rest
of the songs for dissimilar reasons. The first should
appeal to any musical public; the second may prove
too hard a nut to crack for many of even Berlioz's
admirers, though, in the hands of a clever singer with
a sensitive accompanist—the composer thought they
had better be one and the same—much might be made
of this whirlwind of passion. The song was regarded
by Berlioz with something like superstitious awe. As
he says in his Memoirs, 'I believe that I have seldom
been able to attain such poignant truth as in its melodic
accents, plunged in a tempest of sinister harmonies.'
All composers, for intimate reasons, have a predilection
for certain of their compositions. The *Elegy* was composed when Berlioz had returned from the last of his
aimless wanderings some time in January 1830, and,
although in his letter to Ferrand of 7 February he
speaks of his suffering from the absence of Harriet,
I suspect (entirely without evidence) that Camille was
already attracting him in spite of himself, though he
would be loath to hint at this even to his best friend.
He was undergoing a severe mental struggle. That
he commenced his Fantastic Symphony very shortly
after the composition of the *Elegy*, and that the programme of the former was based on his belief in the
affreuses vérités he had heard concerning Harriet, would
seem to bear out my idea. French writers have taken
the 'F.H.S.' that heads the first edition of the *Elegy*
as an abbreviation of 'For Henrietta Smithson', but
F is also the initial letter of Farewell. To quit the
realms of fancy, the *Elegy*, whatever may be the

reason for Berlioz's peculiar regard for it, cannot be numbered amongst his best compositions, if only because the turmoil of his emotions could not be adequately expressed in music. *The Captive*, apart from its melodious merits, is of interest both because it can be considered as a miniature symphonic poem, foreshadowing the methods of Liszt and Strauss, and because it is a good example of the development of a musical thought. The German edition gives three versions. The first, much as it was jotted down in the inn at Subiaco, and sung by Mlle Louise Vernet at the Villa Medici; the second, as sung by Mlle Falcon at Berlioz's concert of 23 November 1834, with a 'cello accompaniment played by Desmarest; the third, in its orchestral shape and practically a new composition, as the composer insisted to Liszt, sung first in London (29 June 1848) by Madame Pauline Viardot.

Of Berlioz's duets for solo voices only one is of real musical value—*The Snare* (*Le Trébuchet*), a delicious little scherzo in 6/8 time for soprano and contralto. With this we may connect two pieces for female chorus in two parts—the *Morning Prayer*, a setting of Lamartine's words, and *The Death of Ophelia*, one of the three numbers included in *Tristia*, the others being the *Religious Meditation* for six-part chorus, and the superb Funeral March for the last scene of *Hamlet*, which is a good example of Saint-Saëns's dictum that no one can imagine the effect of Berlioz's scores from the mere reading. The *Morning Prayer* justifies its subtitle of *Chœur d'enfants* in that it possesses the child-like simplicity of some of Herrick's verses. *The Death of Ophelia* was written originally for a solo voice, and as such figures in vol. xvii of the German edition. It is perhaps a better form for the pathetic melody with its curious wailing refrain, but it contains too many verses, a fault corrected when arranged for a chorus with orchestral accompaniment.

In a previous chapter I have referred to the physical

shock of falling into the Tiber acting as a catalyst which induced a musical reaction in Berlioz. This was in respect of the refrain of *The Fifth of May*. For weeks he had tried to find a melody that satisfied him. Then, two years later, he slipped into the Tiber, and as he dragged himself out, wet and muddy, he realized that he was singing the melody he had previously sought in vain, to the words;

> Pauvre soldat, je reverrai la France ;
> La main d'un fils me fermera les yeux.

(Poor soldier, I shall see France once more ; the hand of a
  son shall close my eyes.)

What particular lady had enthralled him when he had failed to find an appropriate tune, we do not know, but obviously she was not such an effective source of inspiration as the cold bath in Rome. In *A travers chants* he tells the tale, and explains his train of thought. On first falling into the river he felt sure he would drown—he would not 'see France once more !' Then, on discovering that he was in no peril, the revulsion of feeling started 'the inexplicable mechanism within him', and he conceived the melody that expressed his relief. The explanation is simple, but we are no nearer to understanding what the inexplicable mechanism really is. The work, for bass solo, chorus, and orchestra, was first called *The Death of Napoleon*, and was a favourite in Germany. It is certainly worthy of revival.[1] An extract is given in the Treatise, which affords an excellent example of the constant retouches Berlioz gave to his scores. The published score differs from the extract : in the fourth and sixth bars after the division of the double-basses into four, he placed above the D for the two flutes in unison an F and an A for the trumpets, marked $p{=\!=\!=}pp$, without a *sf*. As in his

---

[1] In the full score in the German edition (vol. xiii) there is a serious error of omission in the seventh bar. Here the tempo indication should be 'Moderato ($\bullet = 92$)'. To continue the Larghetto beyond the third pause would be fatal to the music.

arrangement of the Rakoczy March, Berlioz uses the bass drum (specified as 'very large' in the published score) to imitate distant cannon, and marks against the four notes of the part 'Coups de canon loin-tain' as a direction to the drummer, who knowing what he was imitating would be careful to hit his instrument full in the centre, to ensure the requisite deep tone. This has led to a ludicrous mistake in a modern book on orchestration, in which an excerpt is given from the extract in Berlioz's Treatise as an example of the employment of 'the unusual orchestral instrument' a Distant Cannon. If indications are to be confused with instruments, we may expect examples of the use of the unusual orchestral instrument, the Pizzicato.

It is to be deplored that it is not the custom—at any rate in England—to include amongst the orchestral items of a concert short choral works. From a musical point of view they would often be of greater interest than the majority of solos with which we are favoured. *The Fifth of May* is, as I have said, worthy of revival, and—confining ourselves to Berlioz's works—a per-formance of *Sara la baigneuse* by a well-trained choir, proud of its *sotto voce*, should be as successful as it was in 1850. The ballad was composed originally for male quartet, apparently with orchestral accompaniment, for, in a letter to Ferrand of 31 August 1834, Berlioz said that he 'had just finished several pieces for voices and orchestra which will figure, he hopes, in his next concert', which took place on 9 November, when, in addition to *Sara la baigneuse*, *La Belle Voyageuse* (also for male quartet) was given. These two versions are no longer in existence. The latter has reassumed its pristine shape—a song for solo voice, while the former has been cast into two forms—one for three choirs and orchestra, and the other a duet, with the accompaniment arranged from the orchestral score. The ballad in its choral form has some affinity with the Chorus of Sylphs

in *The Damnation of Faust*, and though the Parisian
critics objected that the poem was more fitted for
delivery by a single voice, that need not prevent us
from enjoying the lazy waltz-like melody with its
beautiful termination.

Some have wondered at Berlioz's utilization and
rearrangement of old material. Whatever the reason,
it certainly did not arise from poverty of invention.
There can be no doubt that he composed fluently, but
at the same time was severely self-critical. For the
refrain of *The Fifth of May* we may safely suppose
that he composed a dozen melodies, none of which
satisfied him. That he should have regarded his *prix
de Rome* cantatas and his early or discarded works in
the nature of note-books, from which he could extract
some melody or theme suited to his present purpose,
need cause no surprise—most composers must have
done much the same thing. I would rather insist on
the unerring appropriateness of his selection. The
Harold theme, for example, depicts the character precisely, and yet it had served previously to illustrate
in the first place something connected with Diana
Vernon (in the *Rob Roy* Overture) and then with Marie
Stuart (in a piece for Urhan's *viole d'amour* and afterwards for Paganini's viola—we know nothing definite
in respect to these). To detail Berlioz's employment
of passages that had already appeared in one or other
of his previous works would be beyond the scope of
this book. At times the resemblances between earlier
and later material probably arose unconsciously. Thus,
the second half of the cor anglais solo of *The Roman
Carnival* commences with five bars he had already used
in *Cleopatra*, the fourth one being modified. Here it
is difficult to imagine him deliberately reviewing his
past scores, searching for something wherewith to
continue his melody—we must not forget that what
we know of his early work probably only represents
a tithe of what he had in his portfolios. It is simpler

to believe that, when he composed the love duet in *Benvenuto Cellini* (from which the cor anglais solo is taken), he had penned those five bars before he had realized that he had written them before. A better example is to be found in Cassandra's second air in *The Trojans*, where, as M. Tiersot has pointed out, there are a dozen bars very closely resembling those in the final air of *The Death of Sardanapalus*.[1] Mr. Ernest Newman has remarked on the tendency of composers to express the same or similar ideas in much the same way. And Berlioz, whose style altered little during his career, must have been rather liable to do so. In the above-cited airs both Sardanapalus and Cassandra are reflecting on past happiness which cannot be recaptured. The employment of another theme from the cantata comes in a different category. We cannot imagine Berlioz being inspired by the words of *L'Impériale*, a cantata in praise of Napoleon III. Then he recalls the second air of *Sardanapalus* commencing with the words *Le roi des rois* . . . (again a similarity of sentiment), and, as it fits the words of *L'Impériale*, proceeds to utilize it. He would have cause to remember the theme, for in all likelihood it was the one to which Mendelssohn objected at Rome.

Two of Berlioz's cantatas written in vain attempts to gain the *prix de Rome* are published in the German edition—*Herminia* and *Cleopatra*. The former, as I have said, ought certainly to have won him the prize in 1828. In it we find the first appearance of the *idée fixe* of the Fantastic Symphony, which, as I have suggested elsewhere,[2] was probably part of some composition written during his boyhood, when he was hopelessly enamoured of Estelle. This idea is partly

[1] We do not possess the score of the cantata, but M. Tiersot discovered in the Bibliothèque Nationale in Paris the manuscript of the concluding half of the final air together with the first draft of the orchestral episode that Berlioz added after the cantata had been accepted. (See ' Berlioziana ', *Le Ménestrel*, 16 and 30 Sept. 1906.)

[2] *Berlioz—Four Works.*

corroborated in the cantata itself, for in several passages the words of the poem appear to be forced to fit the theme, instead of the reverse process. From a purely musical point of view the cantata of the preceding year, *The Death of Orpheus*, though exhibiting a greater lack of experience, is better than *Herminia*, in which Berlioz strove to conform to the academic ideas of his examiners. That he should have composed the former after only one year's discipline at the Conservatoire is amazing! The future composer of *The Trojans* had already found himself. That his judges refused him a prize is, however, perfectly understandable, though their excuse, that it was *inexécutable*, was ridiculous. The score is no more complicated than many works of the time, but the pianist chosen to interpret it for the benefit of non-musical members of the jury—and apparently some of the musical ones—was incapable of performing his task. The sub-title of the cantata, *Monologue et bacchanale*, was almost enough to damn the work in the eyes of those who demanded the regulation formal airs. It would be of interest to know how Jean Baptiste Guiraud, the winner of the prize, set the poem. Did his Bacchantes express their regret at having to tear Orpheus to pieces in a ladylike chorus?

The cantata has been given with success at both Paris and Strasburg, but, since it is practically unknown, a somewhat detailed account of it seems necessary. The original manuscript is not in existence, but a copy of it, with three notes in Berlioz's handwriting, was sold to a Marseilles amateur in 1885. The editors of the German edition made attempts to trace that copy, but without success. M. Boschot was more fortunate, and a few years ago found the missing score, which he presented to the Bibliothèque Nationale in Paris. In 1930 the Réunion des Bibliothèques Nationales issued a beautiful photographic reproduction of a copy made by the photographer of the first copy (probably too much ill-used to admit of a clear reproduction), with Berlioz's three autograph notes preserved. The first of these, on the title-page, is a translation of Moore's four-lined verse, of which the last two lines are:

> The sunflower turns on her god, when he sets,
> The same look she turn'd when he rose.

These Berlioz wrote (in English) at the foot of a photograph of himself, which he sent to Mme Fornier (Estelle) forty years later. It is not far-fetched to believe that she inspired the cantata, and that some of the phrases of the Monologue were taken from the love-songs of his boyhood. The second note is the sarcastic one telling how the work declared to be *inexécutable* by the Musical Section of the Institute was *exécuté* on 22 July 1828. As we know, the performance did not actually take place, owing to the illness of Dupont, the tenor. None the less, the rehearsals were sufficient to confound the examiners. The last note refers to the final 'Tableau musical'.

The cantata commences with an Introduction of forty-four bars (Larghetto, the last sixteen being Allegretto) which foreshadows the work. It depicts a scene in the country with the chirpings of birds (a little figure for the first bassoon is labelled 'Turtle-dove') on the wood-wind above a smooth arpeggio accompaniment for the strings. After a dozen bars of Berliozian modulations, it returns to the key of the piece (D major) and there enters the principal theme of the Monologue on the violas in unison with a horn and a couple of flutes. This is followed by an agitated passage in which appears the theme of the Bacchantes, which, in whole or part, is very prominent throughout the cantata.

Ex. 9.

It is a true leitmotiv, and may be considered as the

earliest use of one employed systematically. That there
should be no mistake as to its meaning, the first eight
notes immediately follow Orpheus's first words—
'Prêtresses de Bacchus'. It is absent during the Monologue itself, but appears again in the subsequent recitative, and forms in one shape or another practically the
whole of the accompaniment to the Bacchanal. The
Monologue is an address by Orpheus to his lyre which
in less rhapsodical form Berlioz rewrote as the *Chant
de bonheur* of *Lélio*. Appropriately, the harp and pizzicato strings figure prominently in the accompaniment
in the cantata. Up to the end of the Monologue the
only instruments employed are the usual wood-wind
(with four bassoons), two horns, harp, and strings. It
concludes softly on the common chord of A. It is followed immediately by a fortissimo chord of the minor
9th on the same note for two cornets, two trumpets, two
horns, and three trombones, which is repeated after
two bars' rest by the same instruments forte, but muted,
with 'Écho' marked against their parts. 'Quels cris
affreux', exclaims Orpheus, and we may be certain he
expressed the opinion of the examiners. Here surely
we have the first employment of the cornet,[1] and the
first use of a mute for the trombone; the latter is
usually deemed quite a modern effect. For the Bacchanal kettle-drums and three pairs of cymbals are
added to the orchestra, and the two flutes change to
piccolos. The movement (Allegro assai agitato) is in
C minor, and commences quietly with Orpheus's song
begging Apollo to assist him. The fierce chorus (for
female voices in four parts) of the Bacchantes soon
joins in, and the two run concurrently till Orpheus
expires with 'Eurydice' on his lips. The bloodthirsty
ladies with a cry of Victory on a long-drawn chord
of C major disperse, and we have one of those long

[1] Spontini said in a letter: 'From 1823 to 1831, I sent from Berlin
to Paris a number of piston-horns, and trumpets or cornets with two or
three pistons or valves (the first known in Paris).'

decrescendos, of which Berlioz was fond, ending on a
G for the flute with a C on the 'cellos two octaves and
a fifth below. (Compare the ' Hostias ' of the *Requiem*.)
The score of eighty-two pages ends with a 'Tableau
musical', which is Ex. 34 of the Treatise, a semitone
lower, and in somewhat simpler form. A footnote explains its significance—the wind caressing the strings
of Orpheus's broken lyre, while a Thracian shepherd
attempts to recall the theme of the first song on his
pipe. It may be added that the clarinet is *not* directed
to be enveloped in a bag.

This recently discovered score should make us view
Berlioz from a fresh angle. Although still inexperienced, he was undoubtedly himself as early as 1827. In
the fragment we possess of the early Mass, we have
indeed the germ of the fanfare of the *Requiem*, but
the preceding ' Resurrexit ' is not characteristic—M.
Tiersot finds in it a likeness to Rossini ! In the cantata,
the harmony, modulations, orchestration, melody, and
general conception are truly Berliozian. It was the
only one of his attempts to gain the *prix de Rome* in
which he was himself. In *Herminia* he tried to please
his judges—failing because he could not imagine any
one wishing a prayer to be set as an Allegro con brio;
the greater part of *Cleopatra* was, I fancy, equally
intended to please, but he was unable to resist the
temptation of the realistic touches in the death scene
and the introduction of the Invocation ; for *Sardanapalus* he was also careful, adding the scene of the conflagration only after the cantata was accepted.

Before leaving the cantatas, mention must be made
of a point of interest connected with the prayer in
Herminia. Berlioz had a peculiar affection for it, and,
to save it from oblivion, arranged it for six-part chorus
to words by Gounet, imitated from a poem by Moore.
With piano accompaniment the *Sacred Song* was
included in *Irlande*. Twenty years later it was instrumentated, and was performed apparently for the first

time at Marseilles in December 1843. At Berlioz's concert of 3 February 1844 was given a Hymn for six wind-instruments, two clarinets (soprano and bass), two bugles (large and small), a small trumpet, and a saxophone, all of them recent inventions of Sax. From the notice in *La Gazette musicale* of 11 February 1844 we learn that this was the *Sacred Song*; but how the vocal parts were arranged for the instruments we can only guess. The Hymn was not a success, and was replaced at Berlioz's next concert (on 1 April) by a fantasia of *William Tell*, which probably pleased Sax much more. The interest of the Hymn lies in the fact that Berlioz in all probability was the first composer to employ the saxophone, now alas! so vulgarized, but possessing extraordinary powers of expression, and, controlled by artistic lips, a beauty of tone all its own. Lavoix and the text-books name Kastner as the first to use the instrument, in his biblical opera *Le dernier roi de Juda*. But this was not performed (in concert form) till 1 December, ten months after Berlioz's concert.

The Funeral March for the last scene of *Hamlet* has already been mentioned. It is one of the many compositions of Berlioz that must be heard for its proper appreciation. The composer himself never heard it, for he could never trust himself to conduct it, since he *associated* it with the death of his father. I have italicized the word, because I do not believe that he in any way considered it as a funeral march for his father. Indeed, to connect it with the burial of a quiet country doctor would be inappropriate. The score is dated 'Paris, 22 September 1848', and M. Boschot attributes its inception to a performance of *Hamlet* that Berlioz saw at Riga in May of the preceding year. That may well be, though it is not unlikely that he sketched the march as early as 1827, when he saw Harriet as Ophelia. Dr. Berlioz died on 28 July 1848. The piece is headed by the speech of Fortinbras at the end of the play, and his command, ' Go, bid the soldiers shoot', justifies the direction as to the volley-firing at the culminating point. The chorus—labelled in the French edition merely as 'Femmes et Hommes' —have a small but effective part, merely a series of 'Ahs' at irregular intervals, varying from a sigh or moan to a cry of despair. The end of the march is most impressive. To quote Mr. Christopher Wilson,[1] 'after a terrific triple forte effect, there is a dead silence; then a long, deep, sustained note; then occur about twenty bars of the most hopelessly despairing music I have ever heard, and then the drums take up their dreadful figure, and so the whole march winds to a close. It does not end on any note of hope. There is no thought of a glorious resurrection—all is lost, hopeless, despairing.' As befitting the somewhat military character of the piece, six snare-drums are specified in the score, and these in the French edition are directed to be *sans timbre* (muffled), a highly important indication! Even the most unmusical realize the difference between the typical sharp rattle of the side (snare) drum in its normal condition and the dull sound of the instrument when muffled for a military funeral. The direction is omitted in the German edition, and hence forty-eight bars out of the hundred and eighteen are not as Berlioz wished, and the complexion of the piece is altered.

The first number of *Tristia* is the *Religious Meditation* for six-part chorus and orchestra, on words adapted from Moore. It was composed in Rome in August 1831.[2] From a letter to Hiller of 1 January 1832, it was originally accompanied by seven wind-instruments, and was written one day when the composer was 'dying of the spleen'. He then called the

---

[1] *Shakespeare and Music.*

[2] In both the French and German editions the metronome time is given as a crotchet equalling 54; but in the *33 Mélodies*, in which the chorus is given with an accompaniment for piano, violin, and 'cello, the time is increased to 66.

piece a 'Psalmody for those who have suffered much and whose *soul is sad unto death*'. He had not yet recovered from the blow that Camille had dealt him. Thirty-three years afterwards he told Ferrand that he believed the chorus to be *une chose*—something of merit. One may not entirely agree with him: but the point to which I would draw attention is Berlioz's fondness for setting words of a religious or quasi-religious nature. It is true that we know the *Requiem* and the *Te Deum*, but these are too often criticized from the sensational or dramatic point of view. Even if the religious feeling be grudgingly admitted, it is denounced as being pagan, without regard to the fact that the emotion of a so-called heathen may be as deep and sincere as that of many a Christian. It would be impossible to discriminate between the emotions of an Egyptian maiden kneeling before the shrine of Isis with the infant Horus and those of the same maiden, now converted to Christianity, bowing down before the image of the Virgin and Child, very often economically the self-same image. Christianity, or at any rate medieval Christianity, introduced an emotion absent from many of the older religions, that of terror, and it must be admitted that Berlioz at times was inclined to accentuate this feature. On the other hand, it cannot be said that he neglected other aspects of the Christian creed. That he himself was a free-thinker hardly enters into the question. He had been a pious believer in his boyhood, and it would be no more difficult for him to recall his early impressions than for a staunch Protestant to enter into the feelings of a devout Catholic during the Mass. In chapter xl of the Memoirs Berlioz tells us of the effect that the psalmody of a procession of pilgrims had upon him as a boy of sixteen, when he first experienced that terrible *mal de l'isolement* from which he suffered all his life. In several of his works he introduces a psalmody. He suggests it in the Pilgrims' March, and has one in

Cellini and in the Funeral Procession of Juliet; the two reiterated notes for the chorus in the Offertory carry out the same idea; and I would trace his parlity for monotone in some of his chorus parts to the same cause, such as at the end of the first number of the *Requiem*, and even in secular works like the Chorus of Sylphs and *Sara la baigneuse*.

The *Veni Creator* and the *Tantum ergo* (Ger. ed., vol. vii) are of no value, but the *Hymn for the Consecration of the New Tabernacle* is worthy of mention, if only because we do not usually connect Berlioz with *Hymns Ancient and Modern*. It is a hymn-tune of sixteen bars, and as such could be included in any hymnal.[1] If, as some would have it, Berlioz loved to sup on horrors, he certainly dined more liberally on things appertaining to religion, and he probably derived the habit from Lesueur.

Two more choruses should not be forgotten—the *Hymn to France* and *The Menace of the Franks*, a stirring march that seems to have escaped the attention of bandmasters. As, except for a couple of bars at the end, the voice parts merely double the instrumental ones, the music suffers little from their omission, though the effect is greater when the double chorus (one for male and the other for mixed voices) is employed. As to the arrangement of the orchestral score for military band, from his approval of Wieprecht's arrangement of *Les Francs Juges* Overture for military band, Berlioz had no objection to such a proceeding on occasion. The *Hymn to France*, with its refrain which *La Gazette musicale* declared should become a national proverb, is set to music sufficiently universal to justify the change of title in the German edition to *A Hymn for Fatherland*, though a purist might object that Anglo-

---

[1] The words are by J. H. Vries, a mulatto who came to Paris in 1858, and, under the name of Dr. Noir, was credited with having effected some startling cures. Berlioz followed his treatment for a time, but it afforded him no relief from his *infernales coliques*. Vries was also a religious fanatic, who dreamt of some Tabernacle of marble, which was never built.

Saxons usually associate their native country with their maternal relative. The work, written for one of Berlioz's festival concerts with 1,200 performers, is conceived on the broadest lines and is in reality one long crescendo. The melody is the same for all the verses, sung first by the tenors, then the sopranos, then the basses with the other voices breaking in at times, and finally for the chorus in unison, the accompaniment growing richer with every verse. Berlioz certainly possessed the art of writing for a large number of performers, and yet, on the other hand, he seemed equally capable of expressing himself with the most restricted means, in spite of his remark to Schumann already quoted.

If any work of Berlioz requires to be heard with the ears of the original audience, it is *Lélio*. It contains much good music, but the rhapsodical nature of the monologue seems at times absurd to a modern audience. It must be admitted, however, that, given as Berlioz intended, with a stage setting and a clever actor for the part of Lelio, some of the absurdity is lessened. After all, the rodomontade is no greater than that which is to be found in Hugo's *Hernani*, produced two years before. And, unlike the play, the words of *Lélio* do not appear to have aroused any fierce opposition except maybe from Fétis and his friends, who cannot have enjoyed the diatribe against those 'who dared lay a hand on original works, subjecting them to horrible mutilations, which they called *corrections and improvements, demanding much taste*'. This was in reference to the alterations Fétis had made in Beethoven's symphonies, the words italicized being the critic's own. In scheming the *Monodrame lyrique* Berlioz probably at first intended no more than to carry out the same plan that had proved successful with the Fantastic Symphony—to devise some programme that would enable him to introduce pieces from several sources that he thought worthy of preservation. Amongst those pieces he included the Invocation from *Cleopatra*—the number which had lost him the *prix de Rome* in 1829, and two things from the 'unplayable' cantata *The Death of Orpheus*—a more complicated version of Orpheus's first air, and the instrumental piece. Berlioz flung down the gauntlet to his examiners musically, and some of the monologue was equally defiant. The overture to *The Tempest* (as it was first called) did not receive a fair hearing when it was produced on 7 November 1830, because a real tempest had broken over Paris the same day. So that was included in his hotch-potch, and, as it contains excellent music, it might well be given as a separate item, when a chorus is available. The *Brigands' Song* and *The Fisherman* (with piano accompaniment, to words adapted from Goethe) are the remaining numbers of this strange work. The first is a savage, roystering ditty with little in common with those associated with the brigands of opéra bouffe; the second, in the revised version of the song given in vol. xvii of the German edition, takes a worthy place amongst Berlioz's melodies. It is to be noted, as illustrating the attitude of the audience of 1832, that the prefatory remarks to the *Brigands' Song*, in which Lelio expresses a passionate desire to be one of those outlaws, and the picture of 'distraught women, palpitating with terror ... blood and lagrima-cristi' and such-like, met with applause.

Lélio may be valuable as giving us an insight into Berlioz's state of mind on his return from Italy. But I would rather regard it, as suggested above, as a gesture of defiance to those who had so persistently and so unjustly deprived him of the *prix de Rome*. It was a sort of *Credo*, like his well-known one of later years. He was no longer a student, but a full-fledged musician, and as such was entitled to express his opinions as much as the musical members of the Academy. He attacked Fétis for his attitude towards Beethoven, but most, if not all, of Berlioz's examiners were tarred with the same brush. Even Lesueur, who had been carried away by a performance of the C minor symphony, afterwards changed his opinion of its merits. In any case Berlioz seems to have looked upon *Lélio* as a *pièce d'occasion* with respect to much of the monologue, for he never introduced the Monodrame into any of his concerts till 1855, when in February he gave two concerts at Weimar. In the second of these *Lélio* followed the Fantastic Symphony in its proper stage setting. For the performance he cut the monologue liberally, and introduced many retouches into the music. On the French edition of the score is the mention that this performance at Weimar was the first one. It was apparently the last under Berlioz's direction.

Chapter Seven

THE WORKS

(*continued*)

CONSIDERING that the orchestra is usually taken to
be Berlioz's special domain, it is strange that his
output of purely instrumental music was comparatively so small. Amongst his works there are only
four concert overtures, one of which (that to *Rob Roy*)
he 'burnt'; four symphonies, one largely vocal and
another for military band with a chorus in the finale;
and a couple of marches, one of them afterwards incorporated in a larger work. He also instrumentated the
Marche marocaine of Léopold Meyer, with which the
pianist had delighted the Parisians in the 1840's. In
spite of a commonplace trio there is a certain fascina-
tion in Berlioz's arrangement, for which he wrote a coda
of his own. In truth, his real domain was the opera,
and, but for the failure of *Benvenuto Cellini*, the refusal
of the Opéra to accept the libretto of *Les Francs Juges*,
and the disgraceful way in which he was treated over
La Nonne sanglante, we might have known him principally as an operatic composer. The non-success of
Cellini was without doubt mainly due to the indifferent
libretto, compiled by men with no experience of the
stage. And they were unwise enough to introduce
expressions such as Hugo was employing in his plays,
which were considered inappropriate to the dignified
atmosphere of the Opéra. It is difficult nowadays to
understand any one objecting to Balducci asking his
daughter for his 'hat and stick', but so it was. He
should have demanded his 'mantle and poniard'.
The opera was also encumbered by unnecessary episodes, and some of the scenes were too protracted.
M. Tiersot, in 'Berlioziana', which, by the way, should
certainly be reproduced in book form, gives a detailed
account of the original version of the work, as it exists

in the score preserved in the archives of the Opéra.
The late Charles Malherbe at the time of his death in
1911 was engaged in preparing an edition of the opera
for the German edition. But as neither his co-editor,
nor any one else, has completed his labours, the edition
is still unfinished.[1] In 1876 Berlioz's executors brought
action against the French publishers of *Cellini* and *The
Trojans* to compel them to publish the full scores in
accordance with their agreement with the composer.
The latter pleaded that they were unable to do this,
as under Berlioz's will the autographs were bequeathed
to the Conservatoire, and although Ambroise Thomas
(the then head of the Conservatoire) offered to lend
the manuscripts, the Court pronounced in favour of
the publishers. Had Berlioz been fortunate enough to
be an Italian, with Ricordi as his publisher, we should
have had his operas in the beautiful miniature editions
issued by the firm. But ill luck pursued the French
master, even from his birth!

After the original performances in Paris of *Cellini*
in 1838 Berlioz made no attempt to revise it till Liszt
in 1851 offered to produce it at Weimar. He then at
once set to work to make such alterations as he deemed
necessary, and told his friend in a letter of 29 August
1851: 'I have just examined it seriously, after having
forgotten it for thirteen years, and I swear that I shall
never more recapture that animation and Cellinian
impetuosity, nor such a variety of ideas.' His criticism
was not unsound. There is an extraordinary wealth of
ideas in the opera, and it is strange that we should
witness tinkerings with *The Damnation of Faust* to fit
it for a stage performance, for which it was never intended, when *Cellini* has not yet come into its own.
Berlioz's initial alterations to the opera were by no
means sufficient, and for the Weimar performances

---

[1] M. Masson, in the bibliography to his *Berlioz*, states not only that the
opera is included in the German edition, but that *The Trojans at Carthage*
was published in 1864, which is equally erroneous.

(in March and November 1852) many more were considered necessary. The original two acts were at first expanded into four and then reduced to three, and many scenes were omitted or cut drastically. Unfortunately, here again amateurs were concerned with the libretto. From a letter to his mother of 23 May 1852, we know that Hans von Bülow (then a young man of twenty-two) had much to do with the alterations, which no doubt Berlioz believed emanated entirely from Liszt. Liszt himself must have made some suggestions, and Cornelius, who translated the words, would also have had a finger in the pie. The result achieved by this succession of amateur dramatists does not seem to have militated against the success of the opera in nearly a score of German towns; but, for all that, we still want a version arranged by a practised playwright, aided by a musician who is a conscientious admirer of Berlioz. Although the composer's approval of the Weimar version should have its due weight, it must be remembered that in his anxiety to have the opera produced at all costs he was perhaps too ready to agree to alterations. There is much good music in the original version which ought to be preserved. It is almost unnecessary to add that in any new version no attempt should be made to bring the opera up to date. As Mr. James Agate has wisely observed, speaking more particularly of plays and pictures: 'All good works date.... A work of art dates nobly when it represents the best in its line of its age, ignobly when it doesn't.'[1] For instance, to the audiences of the 1850's there was nothing wrong in the action being delayed, such as it is in the last act by Cellini's air *Sur les monts*. It was deservedly a favourite of Berlioz's, and should be retained. On the other hand, the tenor's air at the commencement of Act II is somewhat indifferent music, and, as it was clearly a sop to the singer, can be cut with advantage. Another sop to the singer is the

[1] *The Sunday Times*, 19 Nov. 1933.

Allegro con fuoco that concludes Teresa's aria in Act 1. Weingartner relates in his *Akkorde* that at one of the performances of the opera which he directed he had determined to cut the Allegro, as being vulgar, when the singer (Frau Herzog) suggested that the tempo was too fast. Ignoring Berlioz's metronome time, the conductor followed the singer's advice, and discovered the true grace of the piece. As it is difficult to believe that Berlioz did not realize the proper tempo, one can only suppose that he marked the rapid tempo to oblige his singer, who would insist on an aria di bravura. The amusing fugued chorus of women pursuing the luckless Fieramosca in Act 1 was abbreviated before the first performance. Now, as M. Boschot has pointed out, it seems too short. And the finale of the opera seems to have been cut too drastically. This and the Carnival Scene are the culminating points of the work, but the whole of it is of interest, even in its present version. Subjected to a reverent revision as outlined above, it should have a new lease of life.

Had Fate allowed Berlioz to become an operatic composer, I doubt whether he would have been a reformer of that branch of music in the sense that Gluck and Wagner were. The conservative vein in Berlioz's musical make-up, backed by his admiration for the operas of Gluck and Spontini's *La Vestale*, would have tended to check any great departure from the then accepted forms. We are, however, safe in saying that Wagner would have found him considerably more difficult to dethrone than Meyerbeer, Rossini, and their imitators. Opera was gradually becoming modified, quite apart from the Bayreuth master, and Berlioz would have had a share in those modifications. *The Damnation of Faust* was never intended for stage representation. The composer, however, at first entitled it *Opéra de concert*, and briefly referred to it in his letters as his opera—a habit that has caused misunderstanding. But much of the part of Faust gives us a clue to what

Berlioz might have done in opera. Faust has one more or less set air, and takes his part in a duet and a trio. On the other hand, the opening scene, that in his study, and the Invocation to Nature are far removed from opera as understood in 1846. In *The Trojans* we find many of the consecrated operatic forms, but they are no longer separate numbers more or less indifferently linked together by recitative. The music flows more continuously. The opera is a series of scenes, in which, by the frequent use of *chant récitatif*—recitative based on song rather than on the inflexions of verbal speech—the old barriers, if not broken down, are often less in evidence.[1] *Beatrice and Benedick*, being an *opéra comique* with spoken dialogue, is on the same lines as those of that date. Berlioz's ideas of opera differed materially from those of Wagner, if only from his objection to making the music 'the humble slave of the words'. This does not mean that he had not an image of the scene constantly before his eyes as he wrote. Any one who has had the privilege of seeing *The Trojans* on the stage will realize how much the music gains in a stage performance. As a matter of fact, Wagner, for all his theories, bears concert performance much better.

That the plan of *The Trojans* is entirely successful cannot be pretended. The opera so obviously consists of two distinct halves, and the one character (Aeneas), who is the sole connecting link between Act I and II ('The Taking of Troy') and Acts III, IV, and V ('The Trojans at Carthage'), has a negligible part in the first half, and is not given the most important role in the second half. Cassandra is the leading character in the former, and Dido in the latter. Berlioz, unconsciously no doubt, did not do justice to Aeneas. In his boyhood he took a dislike to him on account of his treat-

[1] In the vocal scores of *Cellini* and *The Trojans* the indexes have ' Duo ', ' Recit. et Air ', and so on, but this is due to the publishers. In the vocal score of the latter opera, issued in 1889 in conformity with the original manuscript, before the work was split into two, four pages are devoted to descriptions of the various scenes.

ment of Dido, and that dislike swayed him when composing the opera. The hero has some fine music, but on the whole his part is rather a thankless one. In spite, however, of this flaw in the laying-out of the work, it is more satisfactory when given as it was originally written. Berlioz worked out the duration of the opera, and found that, 'if the correct tempi are adopted and well sustained'—again his insistence on the marked indications!—there should be 206 minutes of music, which, with four entr'actes of a quarter of an hour, would mean that the performance would last four hours and twenty-six minutes. Berlioz, however, was not a stage carpenter, and therefore greatly underestimated the time necessary for changing the heavy 'sets'. The performance actually takes over five hours and if the opera is to be given intact, must commence, like *The Twilight of the Gods*, at five in the afternoon.[1]

On the whole *The Trojans* is Berlioz's finest work, though the *Te Deum* (containing perhaps his grandest number) runs it close. As in every composition of large dimensions, there may be a few weak moments in the former, but how many admirable pages there are to counterbalance them! We may not find the 'Cellinian impetuosity' of the earlier opera—it would be misplaced!—but there is a greater variety of ideas. Contrast the delicious little song of Hylas with the humorous duet of the sentinels, the wonderful love duet of Dido and Aeneas with the utterances of Cassandra or the final scene, the quintet, which is finer than the succeeding celebrated septet, with the Royal Hunt. And the entire work contrasts with the charming *Beatrice and Benedick* written shortly afterwards. The

[1] In *Les Troyens de Berlioz* by Étienne Destranges, an interesting analysis of the opera by an admirer of the master, a good many possible cuts are suggested. Absolute repetitions may be at times perhaps superfluous, but Destranges is too anxious to eliminate passages that appear to him out of date (see Mr. Agate's remark above). The cuts that Berlioz suggested, such as the Royal Hunt, are not advisable.

fact that Berlioz was suffering agonies during much of the time in which he was occupied with the composition of the latter, and, as he himself admits, often had no recollection of what he had written the day before, naturally should not affect our judgement of the merits of the music. But it is worthy to be remembered, since it is evidence of the innate musicality of the man. The 'inexplicable mechanism' functioned within him 'in spite of reason', in spite of everything. It is difficult to associate this with the idea of an essentially literary man who dabbled in music in a somewhat amateurish way. An unbiased person might be inclined to agree with Mr. Bernard van Dieren[1] that 'Berlioz was, with the sole exception of Mozart, the composer with the most stupendous native gifts of the last few centuries'. If in nothing else, Berlioz resembled the older master in his variety, and it is this variety that has raised doubts in the minds of his admirers as to which work or number is really his finest achievement.

The Fantastic Symphony has lately been performed so often in England that little need be said regarding it. It has won disciples for the French master, but, on the other hand, has been denounced as a bad symphony, principally because of the first movement, which, according to one writer 'simply breaks the fundamental rules of art, and that not with the iconoclasm of a reformer, but with the awkwardness of a tyro'. If 'breaking the fundamental rules of art' means deviating from the sonata form as laid down by Haydn and Mozart, the accusation is possibly true. If, on the other hand, we take the same writer's definition of form as being that 'which so groups the figures on the canvas as to present them in the best possible relation to each other', the accusation is open to question. It is possible that had we the first movement as originally penned, its 'form' might have been less disputed. The commentary to the symphony in the German

[1] At the Berlioz Conference in Dec. 1928.

edition has thirty-three bars that were cut out by the
composer, and, as these represent merely the beginning
and end of eliminated passages of unknown length, it
is quite probable that he discarded three or more times
that number. As far as can be gathered, they were
concerned with development more or less in Teutonic
fashion, and in the nature of 'note-spinning', to use
the expression of Mr. Ernest Newman in an admirable
article on the work.[1] 'Berlioz did not put together his
music in the conventional German way because he
had not the craftsmanship for it but because it simply
did not appeal to him.' As the critic points out, Berlioz was trying to do what Sibelius has done in our
time, 'sweating all the old superfluous tissue out of
the symphony and making it compact and meaning-
ful throughout.' As already suggested in a previous
chapter, Berlioz in his symphonic compositions strove
after unity. We find that as regards the themes of this
first movement. The first theme, an eight-bar phrase
immediately imitated in the dominant, leads at once
into the melody of the introduction, the same plan as
he adopted in the *King Lear*. The second theme is
intimately attached to the first one by its first two bars
(Min. Sc., p. 18, bars 5 and 6)—the sharpening of the
D is a touch of genius! And the music is seldom far
removed from the three themes. Even the disputed
passage for the strings in the ascending and descending chromatic scales is closely associated with the first
theme by the wail on the wood-wind and horns, which
is derived from the F (sf) and E, the culminating point
of the first phrase of the Allegro. Berlioz, as I have
previously remarked, employed all the artifices of
development, but he did not always employ them in
the place where the academic mind has been taught
to look for them. No doubt there are 'fundamental
rules of art', though it would be extremely difficult
to define them. But, whatever they may be, they are

[1] *The Sunday Times*, 19 Nov. 1933.

certainly not embodied in one particular cast-iron mould. As illustrating Berlioz's feeling for 'form' (the genuine article), it may be noted that the original end of the first movement was abrupt. The string parts were modified on p. 53, bar 6 (Min. Sc.), and then followed by bars 3 to 6 of the next page, concluded by the first chord of bar 7, with the instrumentation somewhat altered. The composer was dissatisfied. He had not grouped his figures so as 'to present them in the best possible relation to each other'. So he added what might be technically termed a coda, yet must be considered not as a tail added to a completed composition in perfect 'form', but rather as an integral part of the form itself. That this completion meant an additional couple of lines to the 'programme' is beside the question, which was a purely musical one. Lelio seeking religious consolation was as good an explanation as the composer could find, when forced to translate his ideas into verbal language.

The 'Romanticism' of the symphony has perhaps been exaggerated. The music is, of course, romantic— all good music reflects the romanticism of its time, and that of the 1830's was of rather an aggressive type —but nevertheless I am inclined to think that our ideas of the music are somewhat swayed by the programme, and the additions made to the music to make it fit the programme. Taking the March as coming from *Les Francs Juges*—a point still disputed by M. Tiersot, which need not be argued here—to illustrate my meaning, in the opera, the March, as far as can be gathered, was probably nothing more than a march of guards, such as is to be found in many operas, possibly conducting a prisoner to be tried by the Vehmgericht.[1] A painful

---

[1] It may be somewhat negative evidence, but surely if the march had been of paramount dramatic importance in the opera, there would have been a place assigned to it in the libretto. There is none. The only indication we have that there was a march is a direction in Act III—'rappel de la Marche', which, by the way, is not irrefutable proof that either the march or its 'rappel' was ever actually written. Berlioz apparently did not

episode no doubt, but not of necessity horrible. In the symphony, thanks to the programme, the march changes its complexion. It is part of an opium dream, and thus, by a stroke of the pen, we are plunged into an atmosphere that would be congenial to Hoffmann, Poe, or Wiertz. Instead of the prisoner being a blameless young man innocent of any crime, he is the murderer of a charming woman and led to the scaffold amidst the execrations of the crowd. Berlioz retouched his march during 'several years', and by the addition of trombone 'pedals' and other means may have sought to bring the music more into conformity with his programme, but for all that I fancy we should hear less of the 'horrors' of the music, if the piece was merely called *Marche des gardes*. The music of the *Sabbat* no doubt might justly be termed 'horrible' in parts, but nevertheless the horror is again due in a measure to the programme. Berlioz, when describing music, at times allowed his pen to run away with him, as is the habit of many other writers. Thus, in *Lélio*, when the artist refers to the march, he talks of executioners, soldiers, and judges. It is difficult to see how the last-named enter into the picture. A better example is the Orgy of the *Harold in Italy* Symphony. After its first performance he describes it to Ferrand as *quelque chose d'un peu violent*. In his open letter to Heine (included in the Memoirs) it has become 'a furious orgy in which are combined the intoxications of wine, blood, joy, and rage . . . in which one laughs, drinks, strikes, destroys, kills, and violates, in short, where one amuses oneself'. As suggested previously, Berlioz may have written with his tongue in his cheek, but at the same time it must be confessed that his description is no more extravagant than many of those written on the music of Wagner, or even Brahms.

The *Harold in Italy* Symphony, although of great

work systematically on the work, but set such scenes as happened to appeal to his mood at the time.

interest, cannot be considered as one of Berlioz's best works, in spite of much charming music. The invention of florid passages for his soloist was not congenial to him, and the intensive study of Beethoven's symphonies he had recently made was to some extent harmful to him. Hailed as a continuator of the German master, he was anxious to prove his affiliation, and so was tempted to essay Teutonic methods which were alien to him. The idea of representing Harold by a theme that remained unchanged by its surroundings was an excellent one. But the task of employing a kind of *cantus firmus* throughout a symphony was not easy. Berlioz dealt with the problem cleverly, but he must have felt relieved to be able legitimately to shelve it for the last movement, even though it meant prefixing it with reminiscences of the preceding movements, imitated from the Ninth Symphony of Beethoven, as some sort of sop for the soloist. The introduction of the Pilgrims' March into the finale, rather foreshadowing *Tannhäuser*, is a happy touch. It should be noted, since it is not to be found in any of the editions, that, according to a letter to Liszt of 7 June 1852, Berlioz wished, when the orchestra was a large one, that the two violins and 'cello 'behind the scenes' should be doubled by a couple of oboes and a bassoon, the former not to play the repeated notes of the psalmody. He also corrected the second violin part in the sixth bar of the march behind the scenes. For the third and fourth beats he substituted E♭ and C for the B♭ and A of the French edition (Min.Sc., p. 195, bar 9). Another point of interest is that towards the end of the first movement Berlioz in his manuscript struck out the repetition of the crescendo passage commencing at bar 4 of p. 65 of the miniature score. That is, he passed from bar 3 of that page to bar 3, p. 71. He must have restored the cut after the rehearsals of the work.

Married in the previous October, 1834 was a busy year for Berlioz, striving to pay off the debts of his wife and himself. During much of the day he must have been running from pillar to post in connexion with his newspapers, and it is a matter for wonder that he managed to compose his symphony in less than two months—the manuscript is dated 'Montmartre, 22 juin 1834'. It is true that he took the *Harold* theme and the second one of the first movement from the *Rob Roy* Overture; and apparently he utilized material from a projected work, *Les derniers instans de Marie Stuart* (at that date attempts were made to drop the final 't' of many French words). *La Gazette musicale* announced this in the previous January, as a fantasia for chorus, orchestra, and solo viola. Nevertheless, he must have worked double tides, often sitting up half the night, since he told Ferrand that on one occasion his pen had not left his hand for thirteen hours at a stretch. Like most 'nervy' people, he was at his best after dusk. Although the symphony, as a whole, may not be up to Berlioz's highest standard, it contains too much that is excellent to be allowed to drop into oblivion.

The *Romeo and Juliet* Symphony, composed five years later, was written under very different conditions. Thanks to Paganini's gift of 20,000 francs—possibly prompted by reasons into which we need not here inquire—for almost the only time in his life Berlioz felt free to devote himself almost exclusively to composition. The form that he adopted for his 'Dramatic' Symphony is open to question, but there is none as to most of the numbers being at a very high level. According to the composer, the musicians of his time were inclined to consider the Love Scene as his finest achievement. It is doubtful whether the opinion would be echoed to-day, even if the indications of the autograph were observed strictly (see next chapter). The present generation, accustomed to the sultry love strains of modern composers, cannot appreciate what might be called a Paul and Virginia love, one that is almost devoid of fleshly passion. We have touched on the chasteness of Berlioz's love music, and it is of interest to remember that in letters to Mme Fornier (Estelle) and the Princess Sayn-Wittgenstein he confesses to the wonderful main theme, which would seem to have affected many composers from Wagner to Gounod, having been inspired by the object of his boyish adoration. The Death Scene, with its permutations of the theme, foreshadows *Tristan*, and, though some may not approve the realism at the end of the number, no one can be deaf to the beautiful Invocation. The delicate scherzo—with the harp harmonics played at the proper pitch—may be deemed a 'standard' work. On the other hand, the pathetic Funeral Procession of Juliet with the psalmody of the chorus on a single note is unknown to modern English audiences. A *complete* performance of the entire symphony is a consummation to be wished. The brilliant Ball Scene is another 'standard' work, obtaining little or no rehearsal, and as such we do not always hear the movement given as the composer intended. The reunion of the two themes, for instance, is at times played fortissimo instead of forte, with the rhythm on the percussion merely *mf*. It is of interest to compare the balance with the reunion of the two themes in the *Cellini* overture, where all the instruments (including the kettle-drums) are marked *ff*, the occasional strokes on the triangle, bass drum, and cymbals being alone only *f*. The difference between the two arises from the different character of the themes. In the symphony the wind instruments have to play their melody with the same melancholy expression as when it was first given by the solo oboe. A fortissimo would obscure this. In the overture, splendour rather than any intimate expressiveness is called for, and hence the theme is performed with the full force of all the brass, which indeed is necessary in order to contend with the powerful effect of the strings in unison and octave.

The finale of the symphony for Friar Laurence,

chorus, and orchestra is sometimes declared to be
'theatrical', the term being used in a derogatory sense.
It is, however, difficult to see how it can be otherwise.
A movement inspired by a scene from a play may be
strictly symphonic; but the actual setting of a scene
must of necessity suggest the stage. Had Berlioz been
writing an opera on the Veronese lovers his finale
would have been the same. Friar Laurence's part
suffers from the fact that he is telling us what we
already know—the same fault is in Shakespeare's play
—but nevertheless it contains much impressive music.
The Oath of Reconciliation must certainly be numbered
amongst Berlioz's best efforts. M. Tiersot would trace
some resemblance between the noble melody and that
of the Pilgrims' Chorus of *Tannhäuser*. That is as
maybe! But, when we hear it intoned by the trombones
beneath the descending scales of the violins, we can
appreciate Liszt's remark to Berlioz on sending a copy
of the overture of Wagner's opera, that he would
recognize something of his own. For the first performance of the work there was a second explanatory
prologue placed immediately after the scherzo. The
music of this has disappeared, though, according to
Stephen Heller, it was of greater interest than that of
the opening prologue.

It is unfortunate that Berlioz wrote his Funeral
and Triumphal Symphony for military band, since
nowadays it is not the custom to introduce one into
concert-rooms. It is true that the work can be given
with greatly reduced means and yet be effective, as
the composer himself proved. But for ordinary concert use many adjustments have to be made. When
Richter gave the symphony in London on 8 June
1885, he had only eight clarinets instead of the thirty-
three marked in the score, and partly atoned for the
deficiency by adding violas to the clarinets. Instead of
such temporary adjustments, dependent on the idio-
syncrasies of particular conductors and the funds of

their managers it is a pity that some composer, skilled in orchestration and an admirer of Berlioz, cannot give us a definite arrangement for symphonic orchestra, such as we have for Wagner's *Huldigungsmarsch*, originally written for military band, and then, after the first eight bars, arranged by Raff for orchestra. Berlioz's symphony aroused the enthusiasm of Wagner, and is undoubtedly one of the composer's best works. The Funeral March that forms the first movement, with its faintly Beethovenish second subject, is a noble composition, containing *inter alia* a wonderful passage on a dominant pedal suggesting an immense procession of a multitude of wailing mourners. The form of the movement was discussed ninety years ago by Maurice Bourges,[1] who asked 'Why should one refuse to M. Berlioz clarity of form (*netteté du plan*)? If there be any confusion, it is evident that it can only exist in the heads of listeners, too prone to judge by appearances.' The second movement, the Funeral Oration, is impressive, given a skilful player of the trombone solo, the longest one written outside some of the forgotten concertos for the instrument. It is strange that Strauss should not have known it, and thus avoided a misunderstanding in his edition of Berlioz's Treatise of the French master's remark that a single trombone in the orchestra was inadvisable. To prove the falsity of such a statement Strauss cites the trombone solo at the commencement of Sachs's monologue. Berlioz, of course, referred to the custom of Cherubini, Méhul, and other composers of their time, of including only one trombone in their orchestra. The last movement, the Apotheosis, preceded by a fanfare, which, though good, is naturally not so grand as that of the *Requiem* intended to convey a different idea, has an irresistible swing about it, which, as Wagner said, the first *gamin* in a blue blouse and red bonnet ought to understand completely. He makes no reservations, and describes the symphony

[1] *La Gazette musicale*, 27 Mar. 342.

as 'grand and noble from the first to the last note'.[1] The work deserves to be widely known, and, under present-day conditions, is unlikely to become so unless we have a conscientious arrangement of it as proposed above.

As every reader knows, Berlioz declared that, if his entire output were threatened with destruction, he would beg that his *Requiem* might be spared. The words occur in a letter to Ferrand of 11 January 1867, and must be taken with a grain of salt. At that time Ricordi was bringing out a second edition of the Italian edition of the *Requiem*, and of course Berlioz had been occupied with the proofs. His mind was full of the work; it was more vivid to him than even *The Trojans*, of which mutilated performances had been given just over three years before. Nevertheless Berlioz had good cause to single out his Op. 5 from his other compositions, since it was the realization of a dream he had long cherished. After the second performance of his Mass on 22 November 1827 he wrote to Ferrand:

'I conducted the orchestra; but, when I saw the picture of the Last Judgement . . . that terrible *clangor tubarum*, those cries of terror of the multitude . . I was seized with a convulsive trembling which I was able to master until the end of the movement, but which forced me to sit down and let the orchestra rest for some minutes; I could not stand upright, and was afraid the bâton would fall from my hand.'

Like Handel, during the composition of the Hallelujah Chorus, Berlioz saw the Heavens open, but, owing probably to his early religious instruction, he was more impressed by the terrors of the damned than the joy of the blessed. His mother had very strong ideas about what happened to those who did not believe as she did. In Rome he schemed an immense composition,

[1] From a letter addressed to a Dresden magazine, and dated 5 May 1841.

M

in which a mock Day of Judgement staged by an Anti-Christ is interrupted by the real one. When he obtained the commission to write a Requiem, to be given with extraordinary means, he foresaw the realization of his dreams, and, to quote his own words, 'fell on the text in a sort of frenzy'. Finding it impossible to jot down his ideas as they arose in his mind quick enough to pin them to paper, he invented a sort of musical shorthand. If any specimens of this are in existence, they would be worthy of publication, though probably they would be unintelligible to all save the composer. The first number is perhaps not appreciated at its full value in the concert-room, when the orchestral forces are displayed before the eyes of the audience. Impatient to hear the 'startling' effects which many of them innocently believe to be Berlioz's essential characteristic, the listeners do not pay full attention to the beauties of the *Requiem et Kyrie*. There is much to be said in favour of a concealed orchestra. The exposure of the complete orchestra is somewhat equivalent to telling the audience of a play what the dénouement will be. The Valhalla theme is more impressive to those ignorant of the disposition of the orchestra of *The Ring*. As C. A. Barry pointed out, in an excellent analysis of the *Requiem*, we must remember that when it is given in a church the several numbers do not follow one another immediately. They are interspersed with prayers, the reading of the Gospel, and so on. These pauses in the music certainly add to its effect. More important is the locale : the cathedral draped in black and lighted only by the candles on the altar ; the black-robed priests and the congregation preserving an attitude of devotion, even if motives other than religious ones have induced their attendance. We may be sure that Berlioz for many passages counted on his *mise-en-scène*, and for that reason the only complete performance he gave, after the initial one, was in the large church of St. Eustache in 1852. As far as I am aware, he included only three of the numbers in his concert programmes—the 'Lachrymosa', by many considered as the finest one of the Mass, although in some respects the 'Rex tremendae' with less popular appeal is finer; the Offertory, in which, above a fugued subject for the orchestra, the choir reiterates with pathetic effect an A and a B♭, only breaking into harmony for the beautiful ending; and the 'Dies irae', with the astounding fanfare for the four orchestras of brass instruments, introduced by that terrific chord of E♭ following a full close in D minor—Berlioz certainly appreciated the value of common chords! The remaining numbers are at the same high level—the 'Sanctus' for tenor solo with the ethereal effect on the violins in their high register, which, if it breathes a pagan spirit, is that of a peculiarly devout pagan, and the following jubilant 'Hosanna'; the unaccompanied 'Quaerens me' in the old ecclesiastical style, and of a calm beauty; and the final 'Agnus Dei', based principally on material already heard in the opening Introit, with a repetition of the trombone pedals of the 'Hostias'.

Perhaps after all Berlioz would have been justified in craving indulgence for his *Requiem*.

The *Te Deum* is a worthy sister of the *Requiem*, and, as a more mature work, may perhaps be considered superior. The religious feeling is more intense. And, if there be any justification for the charge of 'theatricality' as regards the earlier work, there can be none with respect to the later one. Berlioz deemed the 'Judex crederis' his finest creation, and who shall gainsay him? The persistent use of the rhythm of what may be called the 'Judex' motive, first announced on the organ, imparts to the number an extraordinary impression of undefined apprehension. Unfortunately, when the work is given in a concert, we hear it under wrong conditions. Again, Berlioz, when planning the *Te Deum*, had his *mise-en-scène* constantly in his mind. The organ should be at the bottom of the church and the choirs and orchestra at the other extremity of it by the high altar. With this arrangement, the opening chords of the first number, the 'Te Deum laudamus', when the orchestra and organ answer one another, have an arresting effect unobtainable in the concert-room. The form of the number is that of a free double fugue, which .ıas surprised some critics, obsessed by the idea that Berlioz expressed in his writings 'his dislike and contempt for choral fugues'. Strange that his objections to rapid choral fugues on the word *Amen* should be twisted from the particular to the general. The number would seem to justify M. Kœchlin's dictum that 'Berlioz had an innate feeling for counterpoint, though he lacked the thorough knowledge of Bach'. The 'Tibi omnes' is a splendid movement which, in a different vein, is at the same level of inspiration as the 'Judex crederis'. In the autograph score it is followed by an orchestral piece entitled 'Prelude', with a note explaining that it was not to be played except when the *Te Deum* was performed for a thanksgiving after a victory or other service of a military character. It is included in the German edition, but does not appear in the French one for reasons that are obscure. All we know is that in a letter to Liszt (undated, but probably written at the end of April 1855) Berlioz says that he has suppressed the Prelude 'in which the doubtful modulations appear'. In the light of modern practice there is nothing doubtful in the modulations, save to those who profess to find all Berlioz's harmony 'doubtful', and thus we are unable to argue the point; and it would be mere guessing to suggest the name of the objector. We must rest content with possessing a magnificent little tone-poem—it lasts only three minutes—which is worthy of being given apart from the rest of the work. It commences with the rhythm of the theme of the opening number on six muffled snare-drums (described in the first impressions

in the German edition as being *senza tuono preciso*!), and
the theme itself is utilized later.

The following 'Dignare' may not make such an immediate appeal, but none the less in its quiet beauty
it takes high rank amongst Berlioz's works. He himself had a special fondness for it, for he wrote to
Liszt on 1 January 1853—'there is a prayer for two
voices (of the choir) in canonical imitation above this
curious series of pedals held by the other voices of the
choir and the bass instruments:

Ex. 10.

Well sung by the tenors and soprani, I believe that
this number should be pathetic and original. It may
be equally very wearisome. . . .' In *The Childhood of
Christ* he was inclined to believe that Herod's air was
the gem of the work, with the exception of the Duet
at Bethlehem, on account of the technical difficulties he
had to overcome by his use of the Phrygian mode (the
Greek Mixolydian).[1] The 'Dignare' is not wearisome,
and there is a gloomy majesty about Herod's fine air.
But Berlioz, like all musicians, was inclined to have a
fondness for pieces in which he had triumphed over
some purely technical problem. To continue with
the *Te Deum*, the joyful ' Christe, rex gloriae ' affords a
vivid contrast between the preceding 'Dignare' and the

[1] With the exception of Beethoven's Adagio in his fifteenth quartet,
where he employs the Lydian mode, the use of the Greek or Gregorian
scales was unknown amongst composers during the greater part of the nineteenth century. Lesueur pronounced them to be dead. Berlioz employed
them on several occasions, and in this respect may be considered a pioneer.

touching 'Te ergo quaesumus' for tenor solo interrupted by the effective and highly original 'Fiat super
nos' for the soprani of the two choirs accompanied
by soft chords for the cornets and trombones. The
number concludes with a *sotto voce* for all the voices
of the two choirs, in which, by the way, the editors
of the German edition 'correct' an harmonic fault of
the composer's—a 'hidden octave' between an upper
part, moving a semitone, and an inner one, surely not
a grievous offence in five-part harmony. The final
'Judex crederis' must be placed amongst the greatest
movements in music, and it alone should be sufficient to place Berlioz amongst the supreme masters
of the art. It is emphatically one of those movements which illustrate the inadequacy of language to
describe them.

The Childhood of Christ as it now stands requires but
small means for its performance. Originally the material was further restricted, for, in a letter to Liszt of
31 December 1855, Berlioz said that in the score there
were 'only two horns, no trumpets, no cornets, no
third and fourth bassoons, no ophicleides, no percussion instruments [that is, other than the kettle-drums]'.
(It is to be noted that he obviously regarded four
bassoons as being as much an integral part of his
orchestra as four horns.) After the first performances
he added trumpets and cornets to the trombones for
fifteen bars after the savage chorus of the soothsayers
echoing Herod's command for the Massacre of the
Innocents, which concludes the first part of the trilogy.
After a short recitative for the Narrator, it opens with
a Nocturnal March of Roman patrols through the
streets of Jerusalem, interrupted by a duologue for two
centurions discussing the terrors of Herod. Although
interesting and beautifully scored, the march labours
under the disadvantage of being on the now hackneyed
plan of *The Turkish Patrol*, and it is perhaps too long.
Herod's air has been mentioned, and I would draw

attention to the curious incantation of the soothsayers as a proof that Berlioz's excursions into the weird or grotesque did not owe their effect entirely to the employment of extravagant means. It owes much to the harmony, and the weirdness inherent in the musical thought. After the violence of the soothsayers' chorus there could not be any greater contrast than the beautiful duet for Joseph and Mary, which displays a facet of Berlioz's genius too often forgotten, the ability to depict tenderness without drifting into sentimentality. A chorus of angels bidding the pair depart for Egypt concludes the Part. Part II is beyond criticism, with its quaint miniature overture in the Hypodorian mode, the melodious chorus of shepherds, and the charming Repose of the Holy Family, sung by the Narrator. Why are such gems as these so often ignored by the composer's detractors? In Part III, *The Arrival at Saïs*, the Sacred Trilogy becomes more dramatic. Indeed, both it and the first part seem to justify the staging of the whole work at Brussels in 1911. There was on that occasion no difficulty as regards the Narrator, who sang his important part before the curtain until the final unaccompanied number, when he took the stage, backed by the chorus. Part III opens with the Narrator describing the journey of the Holy Family, his *chant récitatif* being based on the theme of the little overture, now in common time instead of 3/4. Then we have the scene of Joseph and Mary, utterly exhausted, seeking shelter for themselves and Child, and being repulsed by Romans and Egyptians as 'vile Hebrews', a reiterated phrase for the violas in their high register being employed with pathetic effect. At last they are succoured by an Ishmaelite, who directs his household to attend to the wants of the poor travellers. The household sets about its duties, its activities being admirably depicted by a free double fugue, of which one subject is in ₵ time, the other in 6/4. Soon there follows a trio for two flutes and a harp, usually performed with the phrasing opposed to Berlioz's indications.[1] At Brussels three children performed an oriental dance consisting mostly of posturing during the trio. After it there is what might be called a 'Goodnight' for the three soloists and chorus, then a short recitative for the Narrator, followed by the *a cappella* final chorus, an unanswerable proof—if proof be needed —that Berlioz required neither an orchestra nor a programme for the expression of his loftiest ideas.

This necessarily inadequate description of *The Childhood of Christ* naturally can convey nothing of the beauty of the work. I have suggested that an approach to Berlioz should be by way of his songs: after the best of them no work can give a better idea of his genius than the Sacred Trilogy. For sheer melodiousness alone it takes a high place, and it is worthy of study from the purely technical point of view.

The Damnation of Faust is, or should be, too well known to need any detailed description. It has been criticized as being a patchwork, and in some respects the charge may be true. But it is a brilliant patchwork, very cunningly pieced together. It is not necessary here to discuss at length the question whether Berlioz ever intended the work for the stage. The principal argument in support of this assumption is a letter from the composer to d'Ortigue of 13 March 1846, in which he says 'tell Dietsch that I am preparing a job for him with my grand opera of Faust. It contains some choruses (*chœurs*) which he must study and carefully polish.' Raoul Gunsbourg, when he produced his distorted version of the work at Monte Carlo in the winter of 1902–3, cited this letter to justify himself. Dietsch, he declared, was conductor at the Opéra, and, to strengthen his argument, he altered the *chœurs* of the

---

[1] In the beautifully engraved miniature score of the work, Berlioz's phrasing is preserved, but the effect of it is at times destroyed by the introduction of breath-pauses, which are neither in the German edition nor in the original folio French one.

letter to *choses* (things). Now, in 1846 Dietsch was
merely the chorus-master at the Opéra, as he was of
several churches. He only became conductor in 1860.
Berlioz at first called his work an *opéra de concert*, and
in his letters at times referred to it as his 'opera'.
His description points to the fact that he wrote for
the concert-room and not the stage. Gunsbourg also
hinted darkly at some page of autograph music (dating
apparently *c.* 1829, the time of the *Eight Scenes* and
the contemplated ballet on Faust), and added to the
programmes for his version an extract from a letter
purporting to be written by Berlioz, which M. Tiersot
unhesitatingly pronounces to be a forgery. No one has
seen the originals of the page of music or the letter.[1]
Strange, how often anything relating to Berlioz is
enveloped in an atmosphere of misrepresentation!
The *Eight Scenes from Faust*, subjected to many alterations and improvements, formed the nucleus of his
later work, and we probably shall not be far wrong if
we connect the Ride and Pandæmonium with the
music written for the Faust ballet. It is regrettable
that Berlioz's biographers in their search for documents should not have unearthed Bohain's scenario of
that ballet. It would throw a light on many points, and
I fancy that we should find that what might be termed
Berlioz's Satanic period was limited to a couple of
years of his life.

Whatever criticism may be brought against the
Dramatic Legend as a whole, there is little that can
be advanced against the separate scenes or the delineation of the three principal characters. The march may
be dragged in, as Berlioz candidly admits in his explanatory preface to the work—an apology that he
afterwards regretted—but its introduction is skilfully

---

[1] The Min. Sc. of *The Damnation of Faust* contains a few directions taken
from Gunsbourg's version. It does not include any of his musical mutilations
and additions. The music is as Berlioz wrote it, save for a 'Hosanna' for
Faust at the end of the Easter Hymn.

prepared, both by its rhythm appearing in the first scene and by the short recitative that prefixes the march, which illustrates Faust's mood. Neither the merriment of the peasants nor martial ardour appeals to him. Surely the opening of the scene in Faust's study, with the passionate cry, '*Oh! je souffre!*', on a discord of the root and 9th in an upper part, wonderfully depicts the seeker groping after unattainable knowledge. To regard Faust's air in Margaret's bedroom as an attempt at a love song would be wrong. He and the girl have met in a dream, and he has been greatly attracted. He *hopes* that he has fallen in love and that that love will give him the peace he has hitherto sought in vain. In his air there is nothing sensual. Even when he sings '*J'aime à contempler ton chevet virginal*' (I love to gaze at thy virginal couch), it is in a hushed whisper, as though contemplating some holy relique, the *sotto voce* of the commencement of the air being here emphatically repeated. At its conclusion he wanders round the room, to one of those long-drawn-out melodies such as could be penned only by Berlioz, examining everything with passionate interest, and we hear again his phrase given out softly on the flute. He is standing by Margaret's bedside.[1] Berlioz quotes the phrase in a letter to Adolphe Samuel of 22 December 1855, commenting, 'Yes! he loves her! But it is not yet then the infinite love of a Romeo, a Shakespearian love. Faust *condescends* to love Margaret; he protects her. Romeo *rises* to the love of Juliet, she is his equal.' Margaret could not possibly hold Faust. As he says in his magnificent Invocation to Nature, 'Thou alone canst give me respite from my unceasing sadness'. We must not look upon Berlioz's Faust as an attempt to depict Goethe's musically. The former, though owing much to the latter,

---

[1] This delicious touch is lost with our English translations. One of them, dating from the 1880's, omits any reference to a bed or couch. In those days it would have been improper. Another translation curiously transforms 'thy virginal couch' into 'my altar of rest'.

has an independent existence. For the benefit of those who are wedded to the idea that Berlioz was unable to resist painting the horrible, I would point out that *his* Faust first sees Margaret in a flowery mead and not in a witches' kitchen, with apes and other monstrosities. His hero, too, is young. There is no hocus-pocus over transmogrifying a lean and slipper'd pantaloon.[1] Berlioz may have found in Faust some likeness to himself, but to take his music as being highly subjective would be wrong. At any rate, he would not have envied the peasants; he would have accompanied their dance on his guitar.

Margaret's portrayal I have already dealt with; and that of Mephistopheles has been accepted as being the most satisfactory delineation of a devil in music, with the possible exception of Liszt's. There is, however, a marked difference between them. While the Hungarian composer's demon confines himself to burlesquing and sneering at Faust's ideas, Berlioz's has an individuality of his own. The Song of the Flea, the Serenade, 'Voici des roses', and his raillery in that wonderfully dramatic scene of the hunt, all help to illustrate Mephistopheles's personality.

Little space is left to comment on the overtures. Amongst them, if we take its original description, should be included the Fantasia on *The Tempest*, the final number of *Lélio*. Berlioz made the alteration partly because it seemed strange to conclude a work with an overture—though there was no reason why Lelio should not have rehearsed one—but principally, I imagine, because he realized that the term 'overture' was a misnomer. It connoted a composition cast in a particular form. That form might be contracted, as with many an operatic overture, or it might be expanded, but in both cases it should possess the same recognizable framework. Berlioz spoke of the *overture*

---

[1] The precise age that Goethe intended his hero to be is open to discussion.

to *Rob Roy*; on his manuscript he wrote 'Intrata di Rob-Roy Mac Gregor'. He was dissatisfied with it, and gave it only one performance, in 1833. He was equally dissatisfied with the overture to *The Tower of Nice* (given in 1845), which afterwards became the overture to *The Corsair*. From the fragments of the former still extant, I am inclined to think that it was on somewhat the same lines as the *Rob Roy*. I have objected to Berlioz being considered as the inventor of the symphonic poem, however much he may have suggested its possibilities. That he did, however, seek for a new form, when he was inspired by some tale, there is little doubt. He realized that 'it is impossible to tell a story in sonata form'. That he was entirely successful cannot be pretended. Nevertheless, the 'fantasia' on *The Tempest*, though not of his best, is worthy of occasional performance: and the 'overture' to *Rob Roy*, though too diffuse, as he himself admitted, is of interest, if only for the employment of the subsequent *Harold* theme. Probably one reason why Berlioz 'burnt' his overture was because he wanted the theme for his symphony, where it received more adequate treatment. Taking them as a whole, and including the noble prelude to *The Trojans at Carthage*, the overtures will bear comparison with those of any composer, both in wealth of ideas and variety.

Berlioz's gifts as a poet must not be forgotten. Many of his verses in his last two operas and *The Childhood of Christ* are of a very high order.

Chapter Eight

INTERPRETATION AND EDITIONS

SUCH was the magnetic character of Berlioz's conducting that Wagner doubted whether any of his works would survive, divorced from his personal direction, with the possible exception of the Funeral and Triumphal Symphony, for which the German master had a whole-hearted admiration. As far as I am aware, Wagner left no record of the French composer's methods, although he had ample opportunity for observing them in Dresden in 1843. Anton Seidl,[1] however, with Cosima Wagner as his informant, has given us a pen-and-ink picture that will serve:

'As conductor of his own compositions he was incomparable. Cosima Wagner has often related how he brought to his rehearsals a tremendous command of the minutiæ of orchestral technics, a wonderful ear for delicate effects and tonal beauty, and an irresistible power of command. Upon all who heard or played under him he exerted an ineradicable influence. His music, frequently rugged in contrasts and daring leaps, is also insinuating and suave at times, and so too was his conducting; one moment he would be high in the air, the next crouched under his desk; one moment he would menace the drummer, and the next flatter the flautist; now he would draw long threads of sound out of the violinists, and anon lunge through the air at the double-basses, or with some daring remark help the violoncellists to draw a cantilena of love-longing out of their thick-bellied instruments. His musicians feared him and his demoniac sarcastic face, and wriggled to escape from his talons.'

There may be some slight exaggeration in the above —his 'demoniac' features would seem to be somewhat belied by his portraits, and the 'fear' of his musicians must have been tempered with admiration for a man

[1] 'Modern Music and Musicians', Part II, vol. i, University Society of New York, 1912.

who drew from them all that was best in them. And we must remember that the description applied more particularly to his conduct *at rehearsal*, with German orchestras, to whom Berlioz, ignorant of their language, would seek to convey his meaning by gesticulation. He indulged in fewer gestures at performance, according to César Cui's account in *La Gazette de Saint-Pétersbourg* of 6 December 1867,[1] on the occasion of Berlioz's second visit to Russia. Cui, after having declared that he preferred Berlioz's conducting of Beethoven to that of Wagner, often finding in the latter affectation and rallentandos of 'dubious sentimentality', continues:

'In regard to his own works, Berlioz, in conducting them, reveals to us a new world, which an assiduous reading of his scores had not enabled us to perceive. From the plastic point of view, what simplicity in the pose, what sobriety and at the same time what precision of gesture !'

Rimsky-Korsakov, in *My Musical Life*, corroborates this, 'Berlioz's beat was simple, clear, beautiful. No vagaries in shading.' He adds, however, that Balakirev told him that at rehearsals Berlioz behaved strangely, that 'he would lose himself and beat three instead of two, or vice versa'. This is not at all improbable. Much the same thing happened at the rehearsals of *The Damnation of Faust* in Vienna two years before, when he had cried to Herbeck (who had conducted the preliminary rehearsals) that he was *malade à mort*. At the performance, however, he was himself again, and conducted with brilliant success. He was equally sick unto death in Russia, and had to drag himself from his bed to attend rehearsals. The 'sobriety of gesture' which Cui observed conflicts with the exuberance described by Seidl. I have, however, partially explained that, and in his younger days, Berlioz may

---

[1] Extracts are given by Octave Fouque in *Les Révolutionnaires de la musique*.

have gesticulated more freely, since Henri Kling,[1] who
saw him conduct in the 1850's says, 'The Master
conducted the chorus and orchestra with very exube-
rant movements of his two arms, and with a beautiful
rhythmic precision.'

Detailed descriptions of Berlioz's methods of conducting are hard to find, though it was universally
agreed that the results were excellent. How he arrived
at them does not now concern us. What is of importance
is his 'beautiful rhythmic precision', i.e. his observance
of strict time. Berlioz undoubtedly meant his indicated
tempo to be closely observed, *and held throughout the
movement*, except where otherwise directed. This
naturally does not mean, as he explains in *The Art of
the Conductor*, that one must follow the indication 'with
the mathematical regularity of a metronome', since
'all music executed under those conditions would be
of a glacial frigidity'. He even doubts 'whether it
would be possible to retain this monotonous uniformity
for more than a limited number of bars'. He wanted
that poised flexibility that Toscanini exhibited in a
Tristan excerpt 'with hardly a moment's deviation from
the tempo of the opening'. Rubato he detested, declaring that it made him feel as though he were dancing
on a slack wire. Over his metronomic indications he
took the greatest care, and in the *33 Mélodies*, published
at the end of his life, we find several numbers and
passages, where he had readjusted the figures he gave
in the original editions—a fact ignored by the editors
of the German one. The idea that, if an interpreter
understands a composer's music, he will instinctively
grasp the correct tempo, is no doubt correct. But a
conductor, for instance, is often called upon to give
performances of works with which he has no great
sympathy, and in that case he wants every assistance
the composer can give him. A moment's reflection
is enough to realize that $\downarrow = 100$ (or whatever the

[1] In *Le Livre d'Or du centenaire d'Hector Berlioz*.

metronomic indication happens to be) is the only *definite* indication in the whole of a score. No system of notation is sufficiently exact to enable a composer to explain the precise accent he requires for a *sfz*, or the degree of force he wishes for a *p* or an *mf*. Slight modifications of the metronome time may occasionally be desirable, depending on the number of performers and the acoustical properties of the concert-hall. Berlioz realized this, when he directed a smaller number of strings for the Queen Mab scherzo, if the orchestra chanced to be a very large one.

On the Berlioz revival in Paris in the 1870's both Saint-Saëns and Reyer objected to some of the tempi adopted by the conductors, simply because they had heard the pieces given under Berlioz himself, and knew that they sounded better at the indicated speed. Later, Saint-Saëns, in a notice of a performance of the *Requiem* at the Trocadéro under Weingartner, sometime during the first decade of the present century, said:

'Never was I able to recapture the impression that the *Tuba mirum* made on me, when I had heard it formerly at Saint-Eustache under Berlioz's direction. This was because the indications of the composer were not strictly observed.'[1]

He then proceeded to explain that the initial tempo is moderato, becoming an andante maestoso on the entry of the four orchestras of brass, when the time is half as slow, two bars of the latter equalling one of the former.[2] He complained that the Andante is often taken as a Moderato,

'and the terrible fanfare, if it does not become, as some one has

---

[1] Reproduced in *École buissonnière*. In *Musical Memories* by Saint-Saëns there is a garbled translation of the above, in which the author is made to declare that the ineffaceable impression of the 'Tuba mirum' was due to Berlioz *not* following his own directions!

[2] The Moderato is marked $\flat = 96$; then, midway through the number *Animez un peu* is indicated, which must be taken to mean a continuous acceleration till $\flat = 144$ is reached at the Andante maestoso, when the tempo drops to $\flat = 72$.

dared to suggest, *un départ pour la chasse*, could well accompany the entrance of a sovereign into his capital, for the composer, in order to give this fanfare a michelangelic character, has not resorted to the facile sombreness of the minor ; it rings out in the splendour of the major, and only a great amplitude in the tempo can preserve its grandiose physiognomy, its impression of terror.'

It may be added that Berlioz evidently took great care over the precise time, since he altered the value of his crotchet for the fanfare from 70, when it appeared first in his early Mass, to 72 in the *Requiem*.

No composer can be indifferent to the tempo of his movements. He calculates his effects on the understanding that his music is to be played at some particular pace, just as a film producer relies on the reel being unwound at a definite speed. Probably Berlioz, with his keen sense of rhythm (in its largest sense) was more solicitous than most composers that his tempi should be strictly observed. And we must not forget that, as with all his other indications, he had many opportunities of testing his metronome figures. Girard's failure to observe the correct times in the *Harold in Italy* Symphony on its first performance decided Berlioz to conduct his works himself in the future. This inability to follow Berlioz's directions is still to be found amongst Parisian conductors, according to M. Maurice Cauchie,[1] who complains of the outrageous speed at which *The Roman Carnival* is usually taken, opposed alike to the clarity of the details and the character of the themes. He wondered at this 'massacre of notes' until he possessed a metronome and found that Berlioz's tempo (156 for the dotted crotchet) corresponded to that which he had worked out for himself. Apparently this unwarranted quickening of the time is not unknown in Germany, if we may trust the 'Philharmonia' edition, in which the duration of the overture is said to be six and a half minutes!

[1] 'Respect for Rhythm', *The Musical Times*, Oct. 1929.

N

As the bars are numbered in the score, it is an easy matter to arrive at the correct duration. It is *eight* and a half minutes—just under five minutes for the two Allegri, and the rest for the Andante. (It is necessary to make this division, since it is obviously possible to obtain the proper duration by dragging the Andante and scurrying the Allegro.)

Other examples might be given, and no doubt some might be adduced by the reader himself, where Berlioz's music has been injured or distorted owing to its being taken at the wrong speed, or by the introduction of unmarked accelerandos and rallentandos. Had Berlioz not been a first-class conductor, or had he published his scores before he had heard a note of them, there might be good reason for seeking to 'improve' them. But an iconoclastic conductor has no such excuses. A good conductor would probably give a better account of one of Ravel's works than that given under the composer's direction. But then M. Ravel does not claim to be a practised *chef d'orchestre*. On the other hand, it is difficult to picture a musician, after having heard a Strauss work under Richard Strauss himself, deliberately presenting it in another fashion, even though his interpretation may be impressed with his own individuality.

It is but a step from conductors to editors. Both should present their composer faithfully. But whereas in the case of the former, errors of judgement or lack of understanding have only a transitory effect, those of editors are preserved in permanent form, and unfortunately there are many who will take the alterations and additions of the editor as emanating from the composer himself, charitably refusing to credit a man with solemnly declaring an edition to be faithful, when he knows the statement to be false. How far a conductor is entitled to make alterations in a score is a nice point that cannot be discussed here. At times, from financial reasons, he may not have control of the

forces the score demands, and therefore is compelled
to effect modifications not anticipated by the composer.
He may not possess four bassoons, and has to make
shift with two. He may achieve excellent results with
his reduced means, but nothing can justify the marking only two bassoons in an edition purporting to be
faithful, if only because another conductor, who *has*
four bassoons at his command, may conscientiously
refrain from employing two of them, believing he is
carrying out the composer's wishes by so doing. If
Dr. Weingartner for performances of *The Damnation of
Faust* elects to substitute for the two ophicleides of the
Drinking Chorus, Trombone I and Tuba, and for the
Amen Fugue, Trombones I and III (playing alter-
nately) and Tuba, we may deplore his choice, but no
irreparable harm is done. To introduce such alterations
into an edition purporting to be faithful is indefensible,
even if the substitution were the universal practice.
But it is by no means universal! Fritz Volbach, in a
footnote to *Das moderne Orchester*, strongly objects
to the substitution, declaring that it is 'inadvisable
(*untunlich*) on account of the totally different tone-
quality'. He himself used two euphoniums (tubas)
for the two ophicleide parts. We may be sure that
a man of Volbach's reputation found many German
conductors to agree with him. Édouard Colonne, who
gave some hundred and fifty performances of *The
Damnation of Faust*, invariably employed two tubas, as
I have a private letter to witness. At the Opéra, where
the number of stage performances of the work is well
over the century, Colonne's example is followed, and
more than probably the custom is general throughout
France.

In *Les Grotesques de la musique* Berlioz tells the story
of an amateur, who approached him after the second
performance of the Legend in Dresden (26 April 1854),
and innocently inquired whether the Amen Fugue
were intended as an irony. Berlioz describes the piece,

with its rapid repetitions of the word Amen to the accompaniment of 'tuba, ophicleide, bassoons, and double basses'. As he was obviously not citing either his manuscript or the French edition, he could only have referred to the disposition of the Dresden orchestra. As we know from his Memoirs that it possessed no ophicleide in 1843, it would be unlikely to include the instrument eleven years later, and he must have deemed himself fortunate to be able to obtain even a single specimen. There was an attempt to revive the ophicleide in Dresden at the commencement of this century, and Klose in 1904 actually wrote a part for it in *Das Leben ein Traum*. But this was merely a flash in the pan. The instrument, though specified by both Wagner and Mendelssohn, was never much cultivated in Germany, and became obsolete three or four decades before it died out in France, where Saint-Saëns in 1877 wrote two parts for it in one of the numbers of *Samson and Delilah*.[1] In 1865, when Berlioz gave *The Damnation of Faust* in Vienna, we may be certain that he would be unable to obtain even a single ophicleide. And we may be equally certain that he did not give the part of the first ophicleide to a trombone (as in the German edition) for the simple reason that it could not play all the notes of the part. Tenor trombones are specified for the work, and are imperative for the 'pedals' marked in the Ride to the Abyss, and the ordinary tenor trombone cannot produce the low E flats of the Drinking Chorus or the D's of the Fugue. Nowadays, in some orchestras the third tenor trombone is armed with an additional piece of tubing operated by a valve worked by the left thumb, but the practice is by no means universal. In any case it is improbable that the first trombone (as in the German

---

[1] The composer directs in a footnote that, should two ophicleides not be procurable, the part of the second is to be taken by a tuba, and that of the first by horns and bassoons in unison, the same combination that Berlioz employs in his fugue to represent a third ophicleide.

edition) would possess the valve. It is as a rule found on the tenor-bass trombone, and not on the true tenor.

This question of substituting one instrument for another is important as regards *any* edition. In an edition of the *Rienzi* Overture the substitution of a tuba for the ophicleide does no great harm, though entirely unnecessary. Conductors are not hopeless idiots, even if it pleases the editors of the German edition of Berlioz to consider them in that light, and they would not hesitate to substitute the modern tuba for the obsolete ophicleide. To replace the serpent in the overture by a tuba would, however, be inexcusable, because opinions are divided about what is the most satisfactory substitute. Yet this is what the editors of the Berlioz edition have done in the case of the fragment from his early Mass. An edition should possess an historical value, and when the Mass was written the tuba had not been invented. It is just as absurd as it would be to substitute saxophones and sarrusophones for some of the instruments in Bach's scores. With regard to the trombones in the Fugue and Drinking Chorus of *The Damnation of Faust* it is not unlikely that the real reason for their appearance may be traced to the fundamental error of the whole of the edition, an insane desire to make it 'practical', that is, equivalent to the 'acting edition' of a play, which possesses only an ephemeral interest. For the modern production of one of Shakespeare's plays the acting edition of David Garrick, or even that of Henry Irving, would be of little use, and neither of them would be of any material value for a study of the original play as written by Shakespeare. Throughout the commentaries to the several volumes the editors of the Berlioz edition harp on the word 'practical' as though it excused every divergence from their author. Yet he, in many cases, is more practical than they. In the *Te Deum*, for instance, since tenor trombones are absolutely imperative for the 'pedals' in the 'Judex crederis', it is surely more *practical* to

specify them as tenor ones that merely to label them
I, II, and III, since, at the date of the edition, the
third instrument in many orchestras would be a bass
trombone, which could not play the notes. Before
dealing with some of the extraordinary methods of
editing displayed in the German edition, I would quote
an extract from a letter from Balakirev to Charles
Malherbe (one of the editors), dated 'St. Petersburg,
12/24 January 1900'.[1] After acknowledging his corre-
spondent's New Year Greetings, the Russian composer goes on:

'The second part of your letter has much disturbed me.
Apparently, instead of fighting tooth and nail for the preservation of Berlioz's instrumentation, you have acquiesced in the
projected changes, since some of the instruments marked in the
scores are no longer in use, and have bowed to the decision of
the publishers, who wish their undertaking to be *practical* [my
italics]. But if the right of editors to alter the instrumentation
in accordance with the actual state of the orchestra be admitted,
it would necessitate the bringing out of fresh scores every fifteen or twenty years.'

The last sentence contains so self-evident a truth that
it is strange that the publishers, if only as business
men, did not realize it. As it is, some of the alterations
of the editors are already as much out of date as Berlioz's original pages. Balakirev then goes on to mention the alto trombone, serpent, and basset-horn, all
of which figure in previous editions of the publishers;
that the double-bassoon had been revived, after having
been neglected for many years; and he points out that
'according to trustworthy evidence' even the ophicleide
was again being employed in the Dresden opera house.
(See above.) And Balakirev was not a *vox clamantis in
deserto*. I could a tale unfold of two English musicians
who protested quite as emphatically. And it is incredible
that there should be only three honest men in Europe!

[1] The whole letter was given by M. Tiersot in the January number of
the *Rivista musicale italiana*, 1930.

It is not a question of whether a man be an admirer of Berlioz : it is merely whether he be an admirer of common honesty and truth. Unfortunately, in France, where one would expect to find the fiercest criticism, the edition was not on sale until many years after it was procurable in England and Germany, and therefore the lips of many musicians who had known Berlioz personally were sealed. Had it been otherwise, it is impossible to believe that Saint-Saëns, for example, who objected to the alterations by Fétis in *L'Africaine*, such as the introduction of saxophones, would not have made some very trenchant remarks about the German edition of Berlioz's works.

It is somewhat of a paradox that, had the late Charles Malherbe been better equipped for his task of editor, he might have brought forward some justification for altering the ophicleides to tubas. In the 1850's Berlioz was anxious to have a uniform edition of his works, and to that end spent some time in correcting the original ones. These corrected scores are now in the Bibliothèque Nationale, and should have been consulted by the editors of any edition, since in many respects they are more authoritative than even the original manuscripts. Lavoix, in his *Histoire de l'instrumentation*, exaggerates when he says that the ophicleides are nearly everywhere (*presque partout*) altered to tubas. In the 1850's the former were in current use in all French orchestras, and Berlioz could not foresee that they would eventually become obsolete. Besides, being accustomed to the ophicleide, he probably preferred it in most cases. In his travels in Germany he seems to have constantly tried to obtain one. Still, the fact remains that here and there in the annotated collection, he did suggest a tuba as an alternative, and so Malherbe, had he known of it, could have offered some shred of an excuse to Balakirev.

As regards the absolute editing of the German edition, there can be little doubt of its having been left practically in the hands of Charles Malherbe, who had easy access to the original manuscripts and the French editions. French musicians have realized this, and it is obvious from the commentaries and scores, wherein there are many things that it would be difficult to connect with Weingartner (his co-editor,) or with any one having much acquaintance with orchestral practice. Weingartner no doubt ran through the proofs, and was probably responsible for some of the more drastic alterations, but I cannot credit him with some of the absurdities. Why Charles Malherbe was selected as an editor is one of the mysteries of the edition. As M. Tiersot said, by way of introduction to Balakirev's letter: 'It is quite certain that Ch. Malherbe, whose principal admirations were confined to Donizetti, Auber, and Weckerlin, was not at all the man to be entrusted with Berlioz. The fact that he possessed some of his autographs conferred on him no claim to figure in an enterprise demanding a sympathetic insight.' With all due deference to Malherbe's memory, M. Tiersot might have gone farther, and declared that he did not possess the requisite knowledge to be the editor of any of the masters, as the publishers of the Rameau edition fully realized when they refrained from entrusting him with the editing of any of Rameau's works. He was an amiable gentleman, whose métier was that of a musico-biographer, for which probably his early training as a lawyer fitted him, and as such he displayed in the prefaces that head the volumes of the Rameau edition extraordinary patience and tireless research. Dr. Weingartner was chosen as an editor, because he, amongst other German conductors, had given brilliant performances of some of Berlioz's works, but, as I would again insist, because a man is an excellent editor of Shakespeare or Bach, it does not at all follow that he could successfully play Hamlet or direct a performance of the B minor Mass. And the converse is equally true.

As an example of Malherbe's unfitness for his task I would instance his alteration of some lucid indications of Berlioz in the first movement of the Fantastic Symphony. For the five bars commencing at p. 4, bar 2, of the Miniature Score, Berlioz marked for the first bar 'poco rallent.', for the next three 'retenu jusqu'au premier mouvement' (omitted in Min. Sc.), and for the last 'un poco ritard.' Simply 'retenu' would be sufficient for the second indication. But there is no obscurity. The tempo has already been quickened (Min. Sc., p. 2, last bar) and is slackened after the culminating point of the violin passage (p. 4, bar 2). To continue the 'rallentando' during the next three bars, where the flute, clarinet, and horn sigh above the arpeggios of the violas and 'cellos, would be irritating for both players and listeners, and therefore Berlioz marked 'retenu', that is, a slower time must be adopted *and maintained*. Then, as the tempo is still faster than the initial one, it must be gradually slowed down to Tempo I. For these carefully considered directions, Malherbe substitutes 'poco rallent. e riten. al Tempo I', which is sheer nonsense, as an attentive study of the first pages of any instruction book would reveal. Neither his co-editor nor any other conductor could beat five bars during which the time was gradually slackened (rallentando) and yet maintained rigidly at the same (slower) pace (ritenuto). If we may trust Liszt's transcription of the symphony, based on the score as it was for the second performance in December 1832,[1] the original indication was merely 'rallentando'. The 'retenu' for the three middle bars was probably

[1] When Liszt brought out a second edition of his transcription in 1876, he only troubled to correct *his* share of the work by modifying some of the fingering, rearranging some of the chords, and so on. He made no attempt to make his version conform with the published orchestral score, even the wording of the programme that heads the symphony not being verbally the same. In the Waltz there are twenty-eight bars at total variance with the piece as we know it, and certain passages in the first movement and March are but poor arrangements of the corresponding ones in Berlioz's final version.

added when Berlioz himself came to conduct the symphony.

Since it seriously affects what is considered by many as Berlioz's finest movement, the Love Scene of the *Romeo and Juliet*, I give another instance of the editing in the German edition, which it is hard to connect with Felix Weingartner. In the second bar after the Allegro that divides the Scene (Min. Sc., p. 151, bar 2) the second violins break off, and Berlioz, wishing them to be muted, marks 'con sordini' in accordance with his usual custom, that is, *before* the bars' rest needed for affixing the mutes, and not on their re-entry, as is the modern method. The indication being above the staff of the second violins is naturally *under*[1] that of the first, and this inevitability appears to have perturbed M. Malherbe greatly. Without a shadow of reason he connects it with the first violins, and plaintively cries, how is it possible to affix a mute and to play a scale? How indeed? An average person would conclude that, as the direction cannot possibly apply to the first violins, it *must* apply to the second. Not so M. Malherbe! He insists that owing to this obscure indication we are forced 'to interpret the author's intentions'—a process that often happens throughout the edition, usually to the disadvantage of the author—and to take 'con sordini' to be 'a general injunction'. (How Berlioz would have smiled!) To carry out this mysterious injunction Malherbe leaves the first violins unmuted (as the composer directs), places mutes on the second violins (again as the composer plainly directs), mutes the violas (which, according to the French score, have never relinquished them), and *mutes the 'cellos*, with the result that, if a conductor is so ill advised as to follow the indication of the German edition, much of the beauty of the movement is

---

[1] The English of the commentary has 'over the part of the first violins'. But this is a mistranslation. The French is *au-dessous*, under. The Miniature Score has the indication placed correctly.

destroyed. Already, before the Allegro, we have had
muted 'cellos, and their peculiar tone-quality is one
that soon palls. To mute them again after the Allegro
is not only an insult to Berlioz's inventiveness and
his keen sense of contrast, it emasculates the passionate
phrases, and tends to produce a monotony that the
movement rightly should not possess.

We are indebted to the German edition for the
publication of the *Heroic Scene* for the first time. It
is unlikely to be performed, but I would cite it here
as another example of Malherbe's mentality which
prompted him, out of two alternatives, to select the
more improbable one. We do not possess the autograph
of the work. In its place we have a beautiful copy,
adorned with a lithograph and vignettes, and elegantly
bound. The finale commences with an Allegro non
troppo ($\textit{d} = 8$o) ¢. Later, the movement becomes a
'precipitate march', following Berlioz's description,
and is labelled Doppio Movimento with a time signature of 2, the principal theme now being in notes of
double the previous length, so that, to the listener, it
sounds precisely the same. Unfortunately the copyist
marked the same metronome time as before ($\textit{d} = 8$o),
which, if only on account of the theme being in notes
of twice the length, would be pronounced by 999
musicians out of 1,000 to be an obvious and not
uncommon error. The editors of the German edition
make precisely the same mistake in the Allegro of *Les
Francs Juges* Overture of adding an unwanted tail to a
semibreve. Charles Malherbe, however, chanced to be
the thousandth man. Claiming a penetration into the
mind of the composer possessed by no one else, he
concluded that Berlioz intended by his indications that
the conductor should *give the impression* of a Doppio
Movimento! To do this, he must beat four in a bar
at the commencement of the finale, and only two in a
bar later. Accordingly, the ¢ of the opening is altered
to C, and the Doppio Movimento struck out and 'Battez

à deux temps' substituted. To justify his proceeding this egregious editor makes the 'infantile assertion' that doubling the time 'alters the character of music'. How its character can be preserved if the main theme 'like a wounded snake drags its slow length along' at half the initial pace he does not explain. The vocal score of the scene retains the indications of the copyist even to the superfluous tail.

It requires a psychiatrist to explain that curious order of mind which, rather than admit that the pen of the copyist may have traced a small unnecessary stroke, prefers to believe that he evolved a Doppio Movimento out of his inner consciousness and wrote some twenty-five erroneous ₵'s. Students of Berlioz must always remember that this strange mentality was not only at the back of the German Berlioz edition, but, on M. Boschot's own confession, was also responsible for every other page of his three-volume biography. In both publications we find the same reluctance to admit the obvious, the same deliberate choice of the more improbable of two alternatives, the same strenuous attempts to justify that choice by the most far-fetched and illogical arguments, at times bordering on the absurd. Musicians have said foolish things; musical literature contains many of them; but, for unadulterated foolishness, few can match the suggestion that a conductor, by beating two instead of four, could give the impression that a theme was being played twice as fast, when, by reason of its being in augmentation, it must inevitably sound twice as slow. It is to be regretted that Felix Weingartner appended his signature to such absurdities.

Charles Malherbe's finger-prints are scattered so freely over all the German edition that it is within the bounds of possibility that the trombones of the Amen Fugue are due to him—his co-editor knew the compass of a tenor trombone. In any case the substitution was probably actuated by the initial fault of the edition, a desire to make it practical, which, being interpreted, meant making it conform to German orchestral practice at the commencement of the century. For the Rakoczy march Berlioz specified an ophicleide and a tuba; the editors have omitted the former, explaining that it is doubtful whether the composer intended 'ophicleide *and* tuba' or 'ophicleide *or* tuba'. Doubtful, when the instruments at the end of the march are in *two* parts ! For the opening of the scene in Auerbach's Cellar Berlioz demanded an ophicleide and a tuba, and they are again in two parts; the editors again omit the former. As we have seen, they save the expense of a second tuba in the Drinking Chorus and Fugue. For seven bars in the Ride to the Abyss an ophicleide and a tuba are in unison; the editors strike out the ophicleide. For the Pandæmonium they do actually mark two tubas, in order to give some faint tinge of colour to their declaration at the end of the commentary as to the 'uniform employment of two Tubas ... throughout the work', which it would be mincing words to call a gross mis-statement.

When his four bassoons were in two parts, Berlioz, in common with other French composers, gave the upper part to 1 and 2, and the lower to 3 and 4 (e.g. for the octaves on pp. 228–9 of the *Romeo and Juliet* Symphony in the Min. Sc.). The editors *at times*— consistency not being one of their virtues—give the upper part to 1 and 3, and the lower to 2 and 4. The effect is the same, but I fail to see the slightest advantage in the plan. Occasionally it leads to confusion, and I mention it here since it is an example of many petty alterations which seem as senseless as they are annoying.

Not only are many of the notes in the German edition not as Berlioz wrote, but, worse still, some of the nuances are changed. The most glaring example of this is in *The Corsair* Overture (Min. Sc., pp. 22 ff.), where the four bassoons (two in the German edition), instead of playing fortissimo throughout, are made to follow the nuances of the upper wood-wind. In the Miniature Score, as in the French edition, p. 17, bar 14, and p. 18, bar 1, are exactly matched by p. 38, bars 11 and 12. In the German edition the *p* in the latter case is omitted, together with the previous diminuendo sign and the subsequent crescendo, with the result that we have a fortissimo passage ending abruptly on a chord marked forte! The excuse given is that the *p* does not figure in the autograph, but was added to the proof of the French edition, which, as the editors themselves point out in their general remarks, was often Berlioz's habit.[1] This inability to appreciate the importance of the composer's own nuances is, alas, not uncommon. Many interpreters appear to imagine that they have done their duty if they give the actual notes correctly, forgetting that in music, as in verbal speech, the meaning of a phrase often depends more on the accents and stresses (the nuances) than on the words or notes. A sentence that to the eye may seem innocent, even laudatory of some one, may on the lips of a speaker be sufficient to damn that some one's reputation.

No doubt many hundred pages in the beautifully engraved German edition conform with Berlioz's wishes. But one has to collate them with those in the French editions, or study the commentaries to the several volumes of the German edition, in which we are at times told what Berlioz really wrote, before one can be assured of their correctness. On the other hand, there are hundreds of other pages not as Berlioz wrote them, which no arguments can justify or excuse. The bad luck that pursued Berlioz all his life is attributed by many to the composer himself, and there may be a certain amount of truth in the assertion. But we cannot hold him responsible either for his biographers or

---

[1] I have discussed these points more fully in ' The Scores of Berlioz and some Modern Editing' (*Musical Times*, Nov. 1915), and in *Berlioz—Four Works*.

for his editors. There are many mysteries connected with the German edition, and possibly the greatest is the apathy displayed towards its very palpable errors even by the French composer's admirers.

There are errors in many of the earlier French editions, but they are mainly errors of engraving, a large proportion of which can be easily corrected. Berlioz, on his own admission, was not a good proof-reader, in that resembling many another author as regards his own works. Nevertheless, he could be trusted to see that the salient points of his score were as he wished them. For his later works he would seem to have obtained the assistance of others. Thus, the careful Deldevez corrected the proofs of *The Damnation of Faust*, and discovered many differences between them and the autograph that had eluded the composer. The miniature scores, apart from a few errors of their own, are faithful copies of the French editions, and as such can be taken as representing Berlioz's wishes.

Whether we shall be ever favoured with a faithful edition of his works is problematical. Should it ever materialize, it is to be hoped that it will be entrusted to men, who have had experience of editing, are in complete sympathy with Berlioz's music, and have made a study of his works. In any case it would be as well if they read chapter xvi of the Memoirs, and learnt by heart Lelio's tirade against arrangers. In the meantime some enterprising publisher might provide us with full scores of *Benvenuto Cellini* and *The Trojans* as Berlioz wrote them. At a price that was not prohibitive surely he would find sufficient subscribers!

Chapter Nine

CONCLUSION

WHAT will be Berlioz's future position in the musical firmament? Are his admirers and detractors to continue for another hundred years their often unseemly bickerings, loudly asserting their opinions without supporting them by any convincing reasons? Of course in some cases it is impossible to give reasons. The most learned musician is in the same boat with the fifth-rate amateur who 'knows what he likes'. If one dislikes this or that melody of Beethoven, Wagner, Berlioz, or Brahms, nothing will convince one of its merits, except on the rare occasions when some gifted interpreter reveals beauties hitherto unsuspected. Perhaps this is oftener the case with Berlioz than with most other composers, because he is so dependent on his times and indications being strictly observed, which less gifted interpreters do not always remember.

No doubt Berlioz profited by the experience of his predecessors, or such of them as were known in Paris in the 1820's, either indirectly through his masters, or directly through his attendance at opera or concert. As I have pointed out, Berlioz was Berlioz (though an inexperienced one) in 1827. But during the six years that had elapsed since his arrival in the capital he must have learnt much from Gluck, Spontini, Kreutzer, Méhul, Catel, and other composers whose names are almost forgotten, if it were only to learn what to avoid. Nevertheless, if we take originality to be essentially a question of apartness, of differing from the rest of mankind in mode of thought, we must certainly admit that the French composer was highly original. And his originality is the more apparent, since his ideas have never become current coinage. He has no direct imitators, who do both good and harm to their model.

On the one hand, minor composers are liable to be influenced by the master some time before he is accepted by the general public, and hence the latter unconsciously grow accustomed to the master's idiom and mode of thought. The way is prepared for him, especially in foreign countries. The French public, for example, had imbibed a good deal of Wagner and water before they were introduced to him undiluted. On the other hand, as suggested in our Chapter I, imitators cheapen a master's originality by copying his methods. Berlioz has been spared the harm, but has been deprived of the advantage, of direct disciples who, as a rule, having served their purpose, are consigned to oblivion. He is almost as much apart from the rest of composers as he was a hundred years ago, and such a man is certain to be unappreciated by many. It is difficult for all of us to understand an order of mind differing from our own; and, if the divergence be great, it is impossible.

Berlioz's originality, his pronounced individuality, will always make much of his music antipathetic to many musicians. I would, however, trace some of the lack of appreciation of his music to the fact that too often he is not treated in the same manner as other composers. I have already complained that, as a man, he is sometimes judged by standards that would be absurd if applied to an ordinary individual. His ideals were as lofty as those of any musician, dead or alive; he was possibly more intensely musical than most; and to him his art was a very sacred thing. Yet in some quarters he is considered as a kind of musical jester, who was not to be taken seriously. This attitude naturally casts doubts on his sincerity, and to have that called into question is fatal for an artist. Whistler was not appreciated by those who agreed with Ruskin that he flung 'a pot of paint in the face of the public'. Many of the peculiarities in modern sculpture would obtain no admirers, if it were believed universally that

o

the artist was seeking notoriety rather than the expression of his own soul.

Theoretically, we should not confuse the artist with the man. In practice most of us do. In the ordinary course we first admire a musician's music, and then are curious to know something of the man himself. And, if the music has appealed to our deepest emotions, we—quite illogically—resent discovering that the composer, as a man, was not on the same level as his music. Illogically, because there is no reason whatever why a musician's life should be any more exemplary than that of a chess player or of a vendor of mechanical toys. Biographers have complied with the wishes of their readers, and, as regards artists in general and perhaps more particularly in respect to musicians, have almost deified their hero. Some modern biographers endeavour to give us the man as he really was, but it is doubtful whether their efforts are always appreciated. Few devout lovers of the Bonn master would agree with Mr. Ernest Newman, when, in a recent article, he says:[1] 'To the eye of commonsense, Beethoven remained to the end of his days what he had been all along, quarrelsome, unjust, arrogant, boorish, decidedly unethical, unspiritual, and undignified.' It is not the place here to discuss the question whether Beethoven as a man possessed god-like qualities or unpleasantly human ones. The point is, if music-lovers had had Mr. Newman's impression of the composer implanted firmly in their minds, would they so readily have perceived divine qualities in his music? It is extremely doubtful! Berlioz's music may be now better known; still, to many, the man is better known than the musician, and many of those who know something of the music have not yet disentangled their picture of the man from their appreciation of his art. The picture is not of necessity displeasing, but it is of one who was incapable of very deep emotion. Perhaps this is the case

[1] *The Sunday Times*, 17 Dec. 1933.

more particularly in England, where there still lingers an impression that the French are essentially frivolous. With our Germanic tendencies, we are disposed to believe some ponderous fallacy of a German philosopher in preference to a witty aphorism of a Voltaire. And it is so in music. Clarity and brilliancy are too often considered as indicative of superficiality, while laboured obscurity is deemed to connote profundity of thought and intensity of feeling.

Saint-Saëns declared that Berlioz did not give a true presentation of himself in the Memoirs. There is no doubt about the strength of his feelings when he is lashing what he considers abuses, the crimes of arrangers, and so forth, but, except occasionally as regards Harriet, he very seldom attempts to reveal the depth of them. Like Figaro, he hastens to laugh lest he should be tempted to weep. Take, for example, the *Épisode bouffon* (the *Drame* of the Memoirs). If Camille and her mother had been living within easy distance of Florence, Berlioz most assuredly would have been guilty of a terrible *crime passionnel*, and slain them both. With his vitality lowered by his quinsy, he was beside himself with rage. Yet of his personal emotions he tells us little. In his story of the episode he dwells mostly on the humorous side of his adventure—his purchases of the feminine garments, how he scared his coachman, his sudden realization that he was famished. Had the episode been written by another hand, these incidents would have been relegated to the background or unmentioned, while Berlioz's remembered happiness and his dreams of its continuance in the future, the horrible suspense he had endured terminated by Mme Moke's abominable letter, the turmoil of his emotions as he set forth on murder bent, would have been very much in the foreground. If I mistake not, to many readers of Berlioz's account of the episode there is an air of unreality which militates against their acceptance of the hero of it as one capable of the deepest emotions or the expression of them. To them the account somewhat resembles the tale of some student's 'rag'. It is difficult for them to realize that the lives of two or three people hung in the balance. Other instances could be given where the charm of Berlioz's prose and his sense of humour combine to conceal his real feelings. If only we possessed the letters he wrote to Ferrand during this crisis in his life, without any doubt we should form a very different estimate of his behaviour at the time. But no matter the reason! The fact remains that to many the picture of the composer that they have formed in their mind is an untrue one, and it is this that prevents them from treating him with the respect that they accord to others, and explains the flippancy with which his music is too often discussed. This erroneous picture of him has been still further distorted by possibly well-meaning biographers who have expended great labour in casting doubts on the veracity of much in the Memoirs, the inaccuracies arising in some cases from a clearly defective memory, in others, as he himself points out, from the tendency of a literary man to slight exaggeration and a desire to round off a story. When, in chapter xxi of the Memoirs, Berlioz says that it was Ferrand who persuaded him to become a critic, he was telling the truth. Berlioz's first article appeared in *Le Corsaire* of 12 August 1823, when the writer was still under age, and there is no reason for doubting that it was his friend, a man somewhat older than himself and already possessing some journalistic experience, who encouraged his maiden effort. Berlioz, however, confuses what happened in 1823 with what occurred five years later, when, in an undated letter,[1] he asked Ferrand for a letter of introduction to a M. d'Eckstein, who was on the staff of a journal shortly to be launched, a thing which a writer of even many years' standing

[1] In the *Lettres intimes* the approximate date—end of 1828—is added by the editor.

might do. The journal was *Le Correspondant*, Berlioz
calling it the *Revue européenne*, which was the title
adopted five years afterwards. His tale, which can be
paralleled by many others, owes its inaccuracy to the
defective memory of a somewhat absent-minded man.
A conscientious biographer must of necessity draw
attention to Berlioz's inaccuracies, which are to be found
even in his private letters, but there are two ways of
doing it, either by treating the whole story as a figment of the composer's brain, or by sympathetically
endeavouring to discover the substratum of truth
which underlies all of them.

Unsympathetic treatment of Berlioz's Memoirs and
writings generally prevents us from obtaining a true
picture of the man. Hippeau points out many inexactitudes in the Memoirs, and, as has been said, is
inclined to rely too much on Legouvé's memory.
Nevertheless, on the whole, he is sympathetic, and
accepts as true several things which M. Boschot, Berlioz's latest biographer, denounces as false. As regards
the latter's three volumes I would quote from a notice
in *The Academy* of 5 September 1908 after the publication of the second volume (*Un Romantique sous
Louis-Philippe*) which would apply to the biography
generally :

'There are moments when one is disposed to accuse M.
Boschot of positive unfairness, so anxious is he to accentuate
all that was weak and ineffectual in the character of Berlioz
the man. . . . Added to this, his lack of sympathy, due apparently to his Mozartian preferences, gives to his painstaking
analysis of Berlioz's conduct at all periods of a combative and
in many respects adventurous life a flavour of acridity, a nag-
ging censoriousness which is intensely irritating, and not a
little contemptible. . . . He lays stress upon his extravagant
gestures and his noisy sentimentality. Much of this might be
said of most men of genius, who have usually managed to make
themselves more or less ridiculous in the ordinary shifts of life.'

It is contemptible ! And if M. Boschot's attitude

arises from an admiration of Mozart, lovers of music should be warned against cultivating such an admiration, for apparently it will not only destroy their sense of justice and fairness, but also ruin any sense of logic that they may possess.

If Haydn or any other composer wrote an Andante in a summer's afternoon, intending it for his fifth quartet, and then, for some reason, did not utilize it for the work, but included it later in his seventh quartet, could he not declare with truth that that Andante was composed in an afternoon ? M. Boschot says not. It is an 'infantile assertion!' All the composer did in an afternoon was to extract some leaves of manuscript music from one of his portfolios. Any one else than a biographer of Berlioz would hesitate before adducing such an absurd *non sequitur*. But the French composer in some mysterious way appears to paralyse the reasoning powers of some of those who discuss him. We have some evidence that the March to Execution was at first intended for *Les Francs Juges*. We have, however, no absolute proof of this. How long Berlioz took to compose the hundred and sixty odd bars of the march in its pristine form (for whatever work it may have been intended) we have no evidence whatever. He says that he composed it in a single night, retouching it for several years, and contrasts the single night with the three weeks he required to compose the Adagio of the Fantastic Symphony, acknowledging that after the first performance he rewrote the latter movement. As we have seen, he did not satisfy himself as regards the refrain of *The Fifth of May* until some years had elapsed. He is candid with respect to his inspirations. And, after all, it is not a very superhuman feat to sketch out on three or four staves during a night of (say) ten hours a march of a hundred and sixty bars, in which several passages are repeated. Sixteen bars an hour ! M. Boschot, however, will have none of this ! He is convinced that the march was originally intended for another work, and therefore a true estimation of the time devoted to its composition, when it was a part of Opus 3, becomes a false one, if it be included in Opus 14. It is difficult to frame a sentence to describe such peculiar arguments!

Again, Berlioz declared that he composed the *Elegy* in a single night, a composition of seventy-one bars, and therefore being probably written at the rate of seven bars an hour.[1] This was after the last of his aimless wanderings through Paris, as we have already noted. He was wrought up to the highest pitch, and surely, for a man with music in his soul, the 'inexplicable mechanism within him' ought then to function. In a footnote M. Boschot seeks to discredit Berlioz's assertion. Might not the *Elegy* have also emanated from *Les Francs Juges*—for which, by the way, it would have been totally unsuited? He endeavours to support his case by citing a letter to Hiller, in which Berlioz remarks that he had used the manuscript of the *Elegy* to relight his fire. Now, the letter was written on 3 March 1830, and, as the *Elegy* was published during the previous month, there was no reason why the autograph need have been preserved.[2] In what way the burning of the manuscript proves that Berlioz was a liar, or that the *Elegy* figured at first in the opera, I leave my readers to decide. When sneering at Berlioz's assertion that his arrangement of the Rakoczy March —originally thirty-two bars shorter—was written in a single night, M. Boschot cries, 'all the orchestral

[1] I have taken ten hours as the length of Berlioz's 'night', since, in a letter to Liszt of 1853, he mentions a march that he had composed on four staves which occupied him till seven o'clock in the morning. He may well have commenced work at nine in the evening. In a letter to Ferrand of 19 March 1834, he says that 'the day before yesterday I wrote for thirteen hours without quitting my pen'.

[2] In the *Correspondance inédite* the letter is dated simply 'Paris 1829', but whether this is due to Berlioz himself, who at times was doubtful even as to the year of the century, or to a somewhat indifferent editor, I do not know. A sentence in the letter tells us the real date, 'It is a year to-day since I saw HER for the last time.' Harriet left Paris on 3 March 1829.

parts being miraculously copied instantaneously!'
Why invoke the aid of miracles, when Berlioz plainly
tells us that the parts were copied in quite a normal
manner at Prague?

There is no particular merit in being able to compose with great rapidity, either in music or literature.
Indeed, the ability to do so may to some extent be
considered a positive disadvantage. The musician or
writer who scribbles with facility is often tempted to
exercise the faculty on occasions when he possesses
no ideas worth recording. Too often, like the tiger to
which Byron compared himself, if he misses with his
first spring, he is unable to take another; in other
words, he is unable to examine critically what he has
written. With him it is a case of hit or miss. A man
engaged in journalism, and the giving and preparation
of concerts, who in ten years composes the works
detailed in Chapter I, cannot be deemed an abnormally
slow worker. And to deny him powers granted will-
ingly to composers of other nations, when we have no
absolute proof of the falsity of his occasional claims,
savours of lack of patriotism, even though M. Boschot
might fiercely resent such an imputation. I have dwelt,
however, on the question, not so much that I am
anxious to suggest the possibility of Berlioz being able
to compose seven bars in sixty minutes, as because
M. Boschot's attitude towards him in this particular
illustrates his attitude in general. And much of this
I attribute to the assistance rendered to the eminent
critic by Charles Malherbe. The insistence that the
title a composer gives a piece affects the time occupied in its composition is of the same order of distorted
thought as the idea that the tempo of a movement
will appear to be quickened, if the conductor beat two
instead of four. It is not without significance that as
regards one detail of Berlioz's life M. Boschot seems
to have altered his opinion, when freed from Malherbe's
influence. In the three-volume biography Berlioz's

account in his letter to Horace Vernet of how, in a moment of weakness, he cast himself into the sea, is scouted as being entirely false. In the valuable chronological and analytical indexes to the volumes the incident is referred to as the 'false suicide'. In *Une Vie romantique* (1919)—an abridged biography—when describing Camille's matrimonial troubles, M. Boschot adds, 'For whom he (Berlioz) had narrowly escaped committing suicide (*failli se suicider*) four years previously'.

Everything conspires to give us a wrong impression of Berlioz, both as a man and a musician. And, like M. Boschot, many musicians take pure assumptions for facts. To account for his ideas on harmony being founded on a different system from their own, they assume that he was lazy during the four years he spent at the Conservatoire. To assert the contrary would be to fall into the same error. Nevertheless, it is quite within the bounds of probability that he worked harder than the majority of the students—he certainly must have blackened more music-paper than most of them. As before suggested, he had not only to correct his own faults, but also those of his masters, if the term can be applied to obsolete rules which the most virulent modern objectors to Berlioz's harmony would never dream of following in their own compositions.

In yet another way we gain a wrong impression of the composer as a musician, and that is as regards the performance of his works. Probably Berlioz was the first composer who placed almost as much stress on *how* his music was performed as on the absolute notes. His predecessors, of course, realized that the meaning of a phrase might vary according to the way in which it was played or sung, and instances might be cited where they endeavoured to convey their wishes as regards performances. But if they had introduced into their scores the indications and nuances with which many modern works are plenteously besprinkled, their orchestras would have been utterly incapable of executing them. For that reason a conductor, provided he follow the broad general outlines, can claim legitimately a good deal of liberty in his interpretation of Haydn or Mozart. With Beethoven his liberty is more restricted, if he would give what the master said, and not what he imagines he might have said. Even in the latter case, unless the conductor's reading approaches the grotesque, as was the sad custom of Hans von Bülow in his later years, we can gather a shrewd idea of Beethoven's meaning. When, however, we come to Berlioz there are many passages in which his meaning escapes us, unless his directions be followed precisely. The speed of the fanfare of the 'Tuba mirum', that Saint-Saëns instanced, is a typical example.

Perhaps where conductors are most liable to err is in the phrasing of his melodies. The editors of the German edition seem inclined to attribute his phrasing at times to carelessness, and, in support of their belief, quote the different slurrings of the theme of the waltz of the Fantastic Symphony on its repetitions. *If* they are the same in the autograph as in the French edition, they may be accounted for in several ways. That in melody, as in harmony, he had not yet found his feet; or that he was attempting a subtlety which he afterwards discarded, that of varying his phrasing on the repetition of a melody, and especially when it was played by other instruments. The latter explanation is not so far-fetched as it may appear. He was undoubtedly fond of making experiments—such as that with the whole-tone scale in *Les Francs Juges* overture—and, as regards the waltz, he does make a marked difference, when he alters the rallentando of the eleventh bar on a repetition of the melody. But whatever may be the explanation of the slurring of the waltz theme, there can be no question that the exact phrasing of his melodies is of paramount importance. Unless we hear them precisely as intended, we have no right to object to them, or, it may be added, to praise them. I would not go quite so far as our

Berliozian authority, Mr. Ernest Newman, who, speaking of the vital distinction between the French master's phrasing of his melodies and that ordinarily given, declared that 'no conductor who is not acutely sensitive to it (the phrasing) can have the slightest understanding of the peculiar build of Berlioz's musical mind, or the slightest right to conduct his works'.[1] Were such a rule enforced we should be deprived of a number of 'half loaves', possibly better than 'no bread'.[2] We ask too much of our conductors. We are content to allow a pianist supreme excellence in the interpretation of a limited number of composers, but we expect our conductors to sympathize with every composer of every school. Parenthetically, every gramophone record should scrupulously conform to the composer's indications, in respect of both the disposition of the orchestra (the proper number of strings and so on), and his directions for nuance, tempo, and phrasing. A record should conform as rigidly to the composer's wishes and intentions as a faithful edition of the score itself.

For several reasons it is difficult to form a true picture of Berlioz. And, although other composers have been the victims of ill luck, few, if any, have experienced such unfair treatment as he. As a man, he certainly receives it in M. Boschot's exhaustive biography, in which, I would add, there are many examples of that flippancy of which I have complained. Too often, in the first volume, the French master, in a patronizing way, is called by his Christian name; there are weak imitations of his prose style in his more rhapsodical vein, with many interpolations of his

---

[1] *The Sunday Times*, 21 Jan. 1934.
[2] For an example of an alteration of Berlioz's phrasing, the curious reader may be referred to the Min. Sc. of the overture to *Benvenuto Cellini*, p. 6, bars 4 ff., where the phrasing is the same as in the French edition. If he will collate the passage with the corresponding one in the German edition, he will be surprised at the differences in the slurring, not only in the melody for the strings, but for the arpeggios for the wood-wind.

occasional expletive—*Feu et tonnerres*; and there is a semi-contemptuous air in so constantly referring to the composer as *notre Jeune-France*, almost equivalent to terming one of our young English composers a Bright Young Thing. If, in a biography of (say) Bach, we had the composer dealt with in similar fashion, and called 'Jack' or 'Johnny', long after he had ceased to be a child, it would be considered bad taste. As a musician, Berlioz has undoubtedly not received fair treatment. Setting aside performances of his works in which his express directions are deliberately ignored or distorted, at the present time (and they will be still more frequent in the future) we have performances in which his wishes are disregarded simply because the conductor has no means of knowing them, unless he consults in some public library the now rare French editions. And, even should he do so, he might reasonably be expected to place more reliance on the German edition, guaranteed by publishers and editors to be absolutely faithful. How is the most conscientious of conductors to know that Berlioz for the *Hamlet* March intended his snare-drums to be muffled? How is he to know that in an important passage in *The Corsair* overture *four* bassoons in unison maintain their fortissimo irrespective of the nuances of the rest of the wood-wind above them? It is true that in the latter case the conductor might consult the miniature score of the work, but its editor is anonymous and does not pledge his honour to the fidelity of the edition. The omission of the number of strings Berlioz required in the German edition is childish, but, except from one point of view, not of vital importance. When a conductor has at his disposal sixty strings or more, for a performance of a Beethoven symphony, he is inclined to double the wind parts. Berlioz, by his indications, tells us that even with a large body of strings he is content with the ordinary wood-wind (with four bassoons).

No one can pretend that Berlioz is adequately

represented by what is now practically the only edition of his works. And he has not received justice in the criticisms of that unfaithful edition. Musicians, who evinced the utmost indignation at the editing of Mussorgsky by Rimsky-Korsakov, and insisted on a new edition of *Boris Godunov*, have not raised the feeblest of protests in respect of the infidelity of the Berlioz edition. Admitting that the alterations of Rimsky-Korsakov are much more sweeping, the principle involved is precisely the same, and I do not know that he ever insisted that he was producing a faithful edition. It is such things as this that go to prove the different treatment Berlioz receives. And until it becomes the custom to criticize him, both as a man and a musician, in the same style as that in which other composers are criticized, we shall never be quit of this wrangling over his merits. His opponents are not entirely to blame. His professed admirers have much to answer for. As is the way with all enthusiasts, they at times allow their enthusiasm to outweigh their discretion, and the more so on account of the adverse criticism the object of their admiration receives. We do not nowadays find the almost hysterical adulation of Wagner's music that existed when it was abused by half the musical world. Where Berlioz's followers are to blame is by too often acquiescing to some extent in many of the charges brought against him—that he commenced his studies too late in life, that in addition he was inclined to be idle at the Conservatoire, that he was dependent on a 'programme' for inspiration, that he placed undue stress on his orchestration. In brief, with many admirers their attitude verges on the apologetic. It is understandable that opponents should compare his ideas on (say) form and melody with what they fondly believe to be the standard one. His admirers should avoid such futile comparisons. Schumann, when contrasting the form of the first movement of the Fantastic Symphony with the classic one, declared that he saw no reason why the one should not be as good as the other. M. Kœchlin, when dealing with Berlioz's harmony, takes up much the same position, which after all is that which we adopt as regards other masters as soon as 'the tumult and the shouting dies'. Berlioz, on the other hand, is judged by the procedure of composers and the rules in the text-books of a hundred years ago. He is said to be without form. Because he is formless? Not at all! Because he strove after a species of form other than that adopted by Mozart and Haydn. And so with his harmony which, unlike that of the vast majority of composers, is not derived from keyboard practice. As regards this point, it is not without significance that the Mannheim School, which was of greater importance in the development of the musical art than perhaps is generally recognized, consisted of men who were violinists rather than clavecinists.

Few of us have a true impression of Berlioz. In the picture we form of him the purples and the shadows are too accentuated. We remember the 'noisy sentimentality' of his somewhat absurd infatuation for Harriet, but forget his healthy normal love for Camille, and his lifelong fealty to his liege-lady Estelle. We think of him as a turbulent young man rather than as one who in middle life was prematurely aged by that agonizing complaint against which he fought so courageously. In music we regard him as the composer of Witches' Sabbaths and Rides to Hell—less than 5 per cent. of his output—instead of the man who wrote *Summer Nights*, *The Childhood of Christ*, and *Beatrice and Benedick*; as a musician who required sixteen kettle-drums and half-a-hundred instruments of brass for the expression of his ideas, rather than one who could produce exquisite miniatures merely with the aid of strings and a few wood-wind. Berlioz was not the unluckiest of mortals, but during his life a larger share of ill luck fell to him than to most of us. Some of this was no doubt due to himself, to his temperament, and to his refusal to depart from his ideals for commercial reasons—a trait that Wagner recognized and admired. For the ill luck that has pursued him since his death he is not responsible.

BIBLIOGRAPHY

Allix, G. *Sur les éléments dont s'est formée la personnalité artistique de Berlioz.* Grenoble, 1903.

Berlioz, H. *Voyage musical en Allemagne et en Italie.* 2 vols. Paris, 1844.

Les Soirées de l'orchestre. Paris, 1852.

Les Grotesques de la musique. Paris, 1859.

A travers chants. Paris, 1862.

Mémoires de Hector Berlioz. Paris, 1870.

Les Musiciens et la musique, with an introduction by André Hallays. (Selected articles by Berlioz.) Paris, 1903.

Correspondance inédite, with an introduction by Daniel Bernard. Paris, 1878.

Lettres intimes, with a preface by Ch. Gounod. Paris, 1882.

Briefe von Hector Berlioz an die Fürstin Carolyne Sayn-Wittgenstein. Leipzig, 1903.

Une page d'amour romantique, letters to Madame Estelle F... Paris, 1903.

Lettres inédites de Hector Berlioz à Thomas Gounet. Grenoble, 1903.

Les Années romantiques (1819–42). Letters collected from all sources by Julien Tiersot, with comments and explanatory notes. Paris, 1907.

Le Musicien errant (1842–52). Letters collected from all sources by Julien Tiersot, with comments and explanatory notes. Paris, 1919.

Au milieu du chemin (1852–5). Paris, 1930.

Briefe an Franz Liszt. 3 vols. (Contains sixty-three letters from Berlioz.) Leipzig, 1903.

Twenty letters to Adolphe Samuel (*Le Ménestrel,* 1879), twenty-six to Auguste Morel and others (*La Revue bleue,* 1912), and many in *La Gazette musicale, Le Guide musical, La Rivista musicale italiana,* &c.

De l'instrumentation, La Gazette musicale, 1844. (Corresponding with the first edition of the Treatise, but without musical examples.)

Grand Traité d'instrumentation et d'orchestration. Nouvelle édition. Paris, n.d. (1856).

Boschot, Adolphe. *La Jeunesse d'un romantique*. Paris, 1906.
Un Romantique sous Louis-Philippe. Paris, 1908.
Le Crépuscule d'un romantique. Paris, 1913. (The three volumes forming a biography of Berlioz.)
Une Vie romantique. (A condensed version of the above.) Paris, 1919.
Le Faust de Berlioz. Paris, 1910.
Chez les musiciens. Paris, 1922.

Brenet, Michel. *Deux pages de la vie de Berlioz*. Paris, 1889.

Cauchie, Maurice. 'Respect for Rhythm' (*The Musical Times*, 1929).

Coquard, Arthur. 'Berlioz' (*Les Musiciens célèbres*). Paris, n.d.

Destranges, Étienne. *Les Troyens de Berlioz*. Paris, 1897.

Edwards, F. G. 'Berlioz in England' (*The Musical Times*, 1903).

Ehlert, Louis. *Lettres sur la musique à une amie* (translated from the German). Paris, 1878.

Ernst, Alfred. *L'Œuvre dramatique de Berlioz*. Paris, 1884.

Feuillet, Georges. *L'Œuvre intense de Berlioz*. Grenoble, 1903.

Fouque, Octave. *Les Révolutionnaires de la musique*. Paris, 1882.

Hadow, W. H. *Studies in Modern Music*, 4th ed., London, 1898.

Hippeau, Edmond. *Berlioz intime*. Paris, 1883.
Berlioz et son temps. Paris, 1890.

Hueffer, Francis. *Half a Century of Music in England*. London, 1889.

Jullien, Adolphe. *Goethe et la musique*. Paris, 1880.
Hector Berlioz, la vie et le combat, les œuvres. Paris, 1882.
Hector Berlioz, sa vie et ses œuvres. Paris, 1888.
Musiciens d'hier et d'aujourd'hui. Paris, 1910.

Kapp, Julius von. *Berlioz*. Contains a useful list of Berlioz's articles, probably founded on Prod'homme's list in the *Zeitschrift der internationalen Musik-Gesellschaft*, fünfter Jahrgang 1903–4. Berlin, 1917.

Kœchlin, Charles. 'Le Cas Berlioz' (*La Revue musicale*, 1922).
Traité de l'harmonie, vol. ii. Paris, 1930.

Lavoix, H. *Les Traducteurs de Shakespeare en musique*. Paris, 1869.
Histoire de l'instrumentation.

L. E. 'Berlioz' (*Temple Bar*, Oct. 1883). The writer, some personal friend of Berlioz, probably Louis Engel.

Legouvé, Ernest. Chapter relating to Berlioz in *Soixante ans de souvenirs* (Paris, 1886), reproduced in *Le Monde musical*, 1903.

Le Livre d'Or du centenaire d'Hector Berlioz, containing appreciations of the master by various musicians, together with an account of the centenary celebrations at La Côte-Saint-André and Grenoble. Grenoble, n.d.

Magnette, Paul. *La Symphonie fantastique*, Liège, 1908.

Mainzer, Joseph. 'M. Berlioz' (*Chronique musical de Paris—* 1re Livraison). Paris, 1838.

Marnold, Jean. 'Hector Berlioz "Musicien"' (*Mercure de France*, 1905).

Masson, Paul Marie. 'Berlioz' (*Les Maîtres de la musique*). Paris, 1923.

Massouges, Georges de. *Berlioz, son œuvre*. Paris, 1870.

Mesnard, Léonce. *Essais de critique musicale. Hector Berlioz–Johannes Brahms*. Paris, 1888.

Mirecourt, Eugène de. *Les Contemporains—Berlioz*. Contains a curiously distorted version of the Camille episode and possibly the first mention of the snuff-box incident. Paris, 1856.

Morillet, Paul. *Berlioz écrivain*. Grenoble, 1903.

Newman, Ernest. *Musical Studies*. London, 1905. Many articles in magazines and newspapers.

Noufflard, Georges. *Hector Berlioz et le mouvement d'art contemporain*. Paris, 1885.

Ortigue, Joseph d'. *Le Balcon de l'Opéra*. Paris, 1833. *Du Théâtre italien et son influence sur le goût musical français*. Paris, 1840.

Pohl, Louise. *Hector Berlioz, Leben und Werke*. Leipzig, 1900.

Pohl, Richard. *Hector Berlioz, Studien und Erinnerungen*. Leipzig, 1884.

Prod'homme, Jacques G. *La Damnation de Faust*. Paris, 1896. *L'Enfance du Christ*. Paris, 1898. *Hector Berlioz*, 1st ed. Paris, 1904. *Hector Berlioz*, 2nd ed. Paris, 1927.

Rey, Étienne. *La Vie amoureuse de Berlioz*. Paris, n.d. (1929).

Reyer, Ernest. *Notes de musique*. Paris, 1875. *Quarante ans de musique*. Paris, n.d.

Rolland, Romain. *Musiciens d'aujourd'hui.* Paris, 1908.

Saint-Saëns, Camille. *Harmonie et mélodie.* Paris, 1885.
Portraits et souvenirs. Paris, n.d. (1903).
École Buissonière. Paris, n.d. (1913).

Schumann, Robert. *Hector Berlioz et Robert Schumann.* Articles by the latter on the former, translated from the German by M. Th. . . .

Tiersot, Julien. *Hector Berlioz et la societé de son temps.* Paris, 1904.
'Berlioziana', a series of articles on Berlioz's works in *Le Ménestrel* of 1904–5.
'Hector Berlioz and Richard Wagner' (*The Musical Quarterly*). Washington, 1917.

Viardot, Paul. *Souvenirs d'un artiste.* Paris, 1910.

Wagner, Richard. *Musiciens, poètes et philosophes,* aperçus et jugements traduits par Camille Benoît. Paris, 1887.

Weingartner, Felix. *On Conducting,* translated by Ernest Newman. Leipzig, 1906.
Akkorde. Leipzig, 1912.
La Symphonie après Beethoven, translated by Mme Camille Chevillard. Paris, n.d. (1899).

Wotton, Tom S. *Hector Berlioz,* a paper read before the Musical Association, 8 December 1903.
'Missverständnisse betreffs Berlioz' (*Die Musik,* December 1903).
Berlioz—Four Works. London, 1929.

INDEX

* *An asterisk prefixed to a title indicates a work projected, destroyed, or surviving in an incomplete form.*